THE MUSIC THEORY OF

GODFREY WINHAM

THE MUSIC THEORY OF
GODFREY WINHAM

Leslie David Blasius

DEPARTMENT OF MUSIC, PRINCETON UNIVERSITY

PRINCETON, NEW JERSEY

Library of Congress Cataloging-in-Publication Data

Blasius, Leslie David, 1955—
    The music theory of Godfrey Winham / Leslie David Blasius.
      p.   cm.
    Contents: Godfrey Winham's conception of music theory—
Selected excerpts—The contents of the Winham archive.
    ISBN 0-691-01227-X (alk. paper)
    1. Winham, Godfrey—Contributions in music theory. 2. Music-
-Theory—20th century. 3. Winham, Godfrey—Archives. I. Title.
MT6.B642M87   1997   97-5562
781'.092—dc21   CIP
                                                        MN

This book has been composed in Palatino

Printed in the United States of America

10 9 8 7 6 5 4 3 2 1

CONTENTS

GODFREY WINHAM: A PERSONAL NOTE

The last time I saw Godfrey Winham, but a few days before his death, I entered the room where he was sitting in bed, a tablet on his lap and a pencil in his hand. It would not have been for him to have been aware of my tentativeness and apprehension, or—at least—to show such awareness. And my apprehensions were mitigated immediately by his vigorous denunciation of a treatment that was worse than the affliction, followed at once by a lively description, in meticulous detail, of his plans for the new composition for computer-synthesized "soprano" voice and computer-generated sound. He wished the "sung" text to express, to state the fact that the voice, like the "language" of the music of the com- puter, was digital in origin, so that the text would be "globally" self-ref- erential. But no poem in the repertory of the only two poets—Hopkins and Shakespeare—whom he admired unreservedly suitably expressed that condition. With a grimace of frustration, he proceeded to what was to become hours of intense conversation about recorded performances to which he had been listening, with detailed questions and—usually— answers about the performances and the works, with—finally—a landing on that still puzzling viola "e" in measure 635 of Schoenberg's *Quartet No. 4;* we had come full, great circle, for it was a well-worn and analyzed copy of that quartet that Godfrey had thrust before me when first we met at Salzburg in 1952, twenty-three years earlier. Godfrey, a proper young Englishman or—at least—a properly clad young Englishman, was appro- priately accompanied by his mother; the two had traveled to Salzburg so that Godfrey could attend the performances of Schoenberg's music; this most un-English interest in Schoenberg surely had been stimulated by two others who had traveled from England to Salzburg: Matyas Seiber, the Hungarian-born composer, who had carried the traditions and tech- niques of the "Second Viennese School" to England in the 1930s, and Hans Keller, the Austrian-born talker and writer on music, who was to become an influential figure at the BBC. Godfrey was studying with both of them: composition with Seiber, and everything with Keller, particular- ly that listening, that analytical "ear-training," which became Keller's cel- ebrated "functional analysis," analysis without words. When Godfrey returned to England it was Keller who transformed Godfrey from an underground prodigy (known for speaking wisely, well, and emphatical- ly at those concerts where observations from the audience were solicited) to a middle-ground prodigy when those who followed the asterisk in the reviews of new music in *The Music Review* found that it disclosed the assigner of evaluative pluses and minuses to be Godfrey Winham, and not the senior critic, Hans Keller.

Godfrey's path to celebrity was diverted when, in 1954, he entered Princeton as an advanced undergraduate, a very advanced undergraduate, who soon advanced on another intellectual front. I remember his first encounter with Nelson Goodman's "The Structure of Appearance," and his proclamation that any intelligent composer who couldn't recognize the profound pertinence of that book to his thinking about music was—well—not so intelligent after all. The lasting consequences of that encounter can be observed in the present study; the immediate consequence was his decision that there were scores to be settled as well as to be composed, and—to that end—his senior thesis at Princeton was "The Logic of Music Criticism." He never wrote explicitly, publicly on that subject, but his few ordinary language reviews were no less logical.

Another of his discoveries at Princeton, whose consequences permanently permeated his thinking, was Schenkerian analysis. Godfrey suffered fools not gladly, but he suffered them, but dilettantes never. He announced that he would not discuss Schenkerian analysis with anyone who had not produced at least one hundred voice-leading sketches. This reduced the universe of discourse to a precious few.

His examination, reexamination, and reconstruction in his own demanding image of the foundations of tonal structure, twelve-tone structure, computer languages, chess, poker, and the world extended even to mathematics. He emerged from school and university with little knowledge of anything that could be viewed as sophisticated mathematics. When he decided he needed mathematics for his work in computer sound production he began from what can be called only an "appreciation" book, and after a few months of his singular brand of exacting study he was using the materials of the functions of a complex variable for his pioneering contributions to digital filter theory; his Fortran program for calculating the Fast Fourier Transform can be found, not in a book on music, but in Steiglitz's "An Introduction to Discrete Systems."

The scope, distinction, and penetrating originality of his creative intellection can be explicitly inferred from this valuable study, and the rich, protean implications, which Godfrey did not live to realize, are also clearly there for those who share his appetites and his abilities, and whose motivation is, as it always was for Godfrey, a musical one, directed to musical ends, by one who was first of all and always a composer, a thinking composer.

Milton Babbitt

INTRODUCTION

Godfrey Winham was born in London, England, in 1934, educated at the Westminster School (1947–51) and the Royal Academy of Music, and studied privately with Matyas Seiber (1952–54). He received his A.B. in music from Princeton University (1956), where he also received an M.F.A. (1958) and was awarded the institution's first Ph.D. in musical composition (1965), with a thesis comprising his *Composition for Orchestra* and an essay entitled "Composition with Arrays." After completing his degree, Dr. Winham remained in Princeton to teach, and (from 1964) became a lecturer and research associate in the field of computer-generated electronic sound. His achievements in this area included the *Music 4B* program (so named to acknowledge both its debt to and its differences from the *Music4* program of Matthews and Miller) for the IBM 7090 and 7094, the *Music4BF* program (with Hubert Howe) for the IBM 360, and the *Music-On-Mini* program for the Hewlett-Packard 2100 minicomputer (with Mark Zuckerman). In collaboration with Kenneth Steiglitz he established a digital-to-analog conversion laboratory at Princeton (1969–70) and undertook pioneering studies of the computer synthesis of speech. He died in Princeton, New Jersey, in 1975.

Although Godfrey Winham published only a few short texts in his lifetime, he was an important member of the ambitious circle of young music theorists trained at Princeton (including such figures as Benjamin Boretz, David Lewin, and James Randall, the latter two being members of Winham's M.F.A. class) who were to leave an important mark on the American musical discourse, contributing in particular to the establishment of music theory as an autonomous discipline. He left behind an extraordinary collection of writings on music theory, philosophy, logic, literary criticism, chess, poker, invented games, the computer synthesis of sound, speech and music, and other more general intellectual concerns. The musical writings comprise over half of these papers (approximately forty-six hundred pages of text and perhaps another seven hundred leaves of writings on score paper). These musical writings, together with a typewritten transcript (or xerox where appropriate) and an editorial volume containing both a comprehensive descriptive table of contents and various indexes, are permanently held in the Special Collections of the Firestone Library at Princeton University. (The transcription was done after his death in 1975 by Bethany Winham, and was subsequently edited and indexed by Roger Maren in 1980–81.) These writings are organized into three categories. In the first are those manuscripts written in pencil on what are now separate sheets of lined notebook paper. These papers have been grouped in folders according (at least to a great extent) to how they were found at the time of Winham's death: it can be assumed that in many of these cases these separate sheets were collated by the author himself. In the second category are forty-three spiral-bound notebooks, again written in pencil. In the third category are notebooks and collated individual pages written on score paper, most of which is in musical notation. The first category of manuscripts are assigned by the editor with the designation of an asterisk followed by a numeral, sometimes subcategorized by a letter, and given page numbers (i.e., *26a: 17). The notebooks are assigned the designation "N" and page numbers (i.e., N17: 4–7). The folders of manuscripts on score paper are marked by a numeral preceded by the designation "S" and again assigned page numbers (i.e., S10: 3).

In terms of content, the manuscripts themselves comprise what seem to be drafts for articles, working notes, occasional notes (for meetings or classes), drafts of correspondence, outlines for books, and other materials. Many of the notebooks have a thematic consistency; it seems apparent that Winham would allot particular notebooks to particular topics, adding to them as the circumstances required. Likewise, a number of the folders are thematically consistent (although we would not make too much of this consistency; some of the folders gather odd materials found by the transcriber and editor).

The style of writing in the manuscripts is always clear and concise. In fact, if clarity of language was the sole criteria, much of this material could be published as it stands: thus in this study I found that I need not have any reservations about quoting Winham at length. But in fact, one feels that little of this material would be immediately publishable in its present form. Only a small percentage of this material is trivial (in the sense of being personal or class notes); thus it would appear that a large majority was penned with an eye to eventual publication. But almost all of it is incomplete. Drafts of articles or essays or talks at times break off abruptly, at times simply tail off. More important, though, while Winham holds to certain central themes, certain important ideas, these themes or ideas are subject to a constant process of restatement and refinement, a constant search for precision and definition and consistency.

Thus, it is almost impossible to specify with certainty what Winham would have accepted as a definitive statement of any particular idea: indeed, one is on safe ground in venturing that such definitive statements are not to be found in these papers. Even the notion of a chronology is suspect. Beyond noting that most of this material dates from the mid- to late 1960s (most of the notebooks themselves were purchased between 1964 and 1966), there is little physical evidence of use in dating the manuscripts. One cannot escape noticing that certain materials predate other materials. But it would be difficult if not impossible to determine even a rough chronology, or even in most cases to construct some manner of topical stemma. (The numbering of the manuscripts cannot, of course, be taken to indicate a chronology.)

These conditions have determined the form and procedures of this study. It has three parts—the first, an extended essay; the second, a gathering of ten excerpts (when the particular excerpt is cited in the essay, this has been noted); and the third, a reproduction of the table of contents of the archive.

Because, simply, of the sheer number of different ideas and projects found in the archive, I have not made an effort in my essay and in the selection of excerpts to give a comprehensive accounting of the material therein. (The range of Winham's interests is made clear by the table of contents in Part 3.) My essay focuses on those materials that I have found most interesting and central to his agenda, specifically on Winham's metatheory (his speculations on the construction of an axiomaticized theory of music and his attempts at an analysis of tonal music). I have therefore not given any consideration to those materials that deal with twelve-tone theory, or given much consideration to those passages that seem more critical, personal, or ideological than theoretically substantive. Nor have I given any extended treatment of Winham's analytic sketches. In regard to the first omission, I feel that Winham's dissertation, published in *Perspectives on New Music* as "A Theory of Arrays," does more than suffice to give an adequate introduction to (at least one aspect of) his compositional thinking. In regard to the second omission, it strikes me that many of the issues that (at times) preoccupy Winham—the conflict, as such, between "radical" and "conservative" composers, the "crisis" in musical pedagogy, advertising as a root cause of problems in American society, etc.—are (even more directly than his music theory) the products of a particular place and time, and hence are not of more than historical interest to us today. The third omission is the one I regret most. A considerable portion of Winham's work consisted of the sustained and insightful examination of musical texts, an analytic practice striking in its subtlety. Winham's sketches are of intrinsic interest. Yet because of the nature of his agenda, the process of analysis is increasingly bound up with questions as to the domain of music theory, the nature of its claims, and the ways in which the analysis of texts is determined or undetermined by these claims, and therefore I believe that some sense of his analytic style and concerns comes across in this study.

Several additional remarks are in order. First, I have attempted to use a wide selection of texts inasmuch as they apply to particular problems in the discussion: these are always referenced by manuscript and page number. Second, there is a certain amount of technical philosophy contained in this essay. Particularly in the opening sections wherein I lay out some of Winham's thoughts on such notions as the definition of the musical score and the musical work, the distinction between analysis and description, and the definition of musical structure, some knowledge of analytic philosophy may prove of value. (I think of such things as the distinction between syntactic and semantic systems.) Later sections of the essay, though, in truth require no such knowledge. In the case of the logical formulae contained in this essay, I have given (in one instance) Winham's interpretations and (in the other case) the interpretations found in the original work of Carnap drawn on by Winham. Third, in the interest of a narrative synthesis I have extrapolated certain ties between seemingly unconnected works (particularly in regard to Winham's construction of musical time). I have also rather loosely used the work *phenomenology* in reference to certain explanations. This is not a term Dr. Winham uses, and the locution *phenomenalistic construction* might be more accurate (inasmuch as these explications take as their subject musical phenomena and as their method Carnap's axiomatic constructivism), yet I find the use of phenomenology less awkward. No connection is to be drawn with the analysis of continental phenomenology.

Finally, this study was born of mixed motivations. The concerns of Winham's music theory are undeniably removed (to a certain extent) from our own, and one is tempted to regard his writings as being of a strictly historical interest. His writings are without question an artifact of their times, of a particular exuberance for the possibilities of a "scientific" or at least epistemologically secure musical discourse. They are a record of a moment when music theory sought to separate itself from historical musicology and (in alliance with the compositional theorizing of the time) gain a disciplinary and institutional autonomy. (Thus there is only a glancing acknowledgment of the history of music theory in Dr. Winham's writings, and no sense of historicism.) In this regard, the material in the archives is extremely valuable, revealing a range of theorizing that (in retrospect) we might have forgotten and demonstrating the diversity and individuality possible within the ideology of a scientific music theory. Winham assumes many theoretical stances that are at odds with those taken by his better-known colleagues, and supports them through very close argument.

Yet having entered Winham's universe, one becomes caught up in his concerns, and one becomes less sure of the historical distance that separates our world and his. In a sense, the questions with which he wrestles are still germane and still unresolved.

Perhaps the best way, though, to approach the material in these archives is to hold these characterizations in abeyance. Thus it is hoped that Godfrey Winham in my essay will speak for himself. The Winham revealed in his papers is (in many ways) a deeply conservative figure quite honestly and openly dealing with an increasingly radical discourse. Although he quite accurately points out the flawed reasoning underlying received theory and analysis, he believes in the stuff of that theory and analysis, in scales and modes, and consonance and triadic harmony, and in the canon of great works. He is uncomfortable with the relativistic universe unfolding around him, one in which any number of musical systems are possible, and any number of musical analyses valid. Thus his appropriation of all of the arcana of technical philosophy is not an act of arrogance or hubris but rather a strategy through which he attempts to establish some manner of discursive stability. Thus his singular achievement is the sort of terrible honesty with which he attempts (and ultimately abandons) the project. His work may lead us to question our own presuppositions about music theory and analysis as a discipline, but perhaps most important, it may provide a benchmark against which we can measure the honesty with which we test our presuppositions. For this reason, it is hoped that my work will not stand alone but serve as an incentive for others to explore the Winham archive.

In putting together this study, I have been indebted to a number of people. Bethany Winham supported this project financially. More important, though, it was her labor in the transcription of Dr. Winham's papers (an enormous task) that made their preservation in the Winham archive possible. Also, my work would have been almost impossible without the table of contents and the index of this material prepared by Roger Maren: these tools will prove invaluable for any future study of these papers. I must certainly thank Professor James Randall for sharing his reminiscences, and must also thank the Department of Music at Princeton University for supporting the publication of this volume. Last, I would be remiss in not acknowledging the role played by the late Arthur Komar in this project. Professor Komar worked extensively with Godfrey Winham during his graduate studies at Princeton, and his dissertation was (as he acknowledged) deeply indebted to many of Winham's ideas. When Arthur decided to start his own publishing venture, Ovenbird Press, he immediately thought to commission this study of Dr. Winham's ideas. In the course of my work, he was not simply a source of guidance but also of continuing moral support (a necessary resource for any author). I deeply regret that he did not live to see the completion of this study, which I dedicate to his memory.

Godfrey Winham
(London, England, 1951)

GwenWinham,
Godfrey's mother (Belle
Mead, New Jersey,
1967)

Godfrey Winham in a chess tournament (Asbury Park, New Jersey, 1960)

Godfrey Winham and Bethany Beardslee (New York, New York, 1955)

Godfrey Winham and
Milton Babbitt
(Princeton, New Jersey,
1965)

Godfrey Winham and Arthur
Komar (Belle Mead, New
Jersey, 1966)

THE MUSIC THEORY OF
GODFREY WINHAM

PART 1

Godfrey Winham's Conception of Music Theory

The Problem of Musical Significance

The music theory that comes into being in the late 1950s and through the 1960s is the product of various factors unique to that moment in the American academy. Among these, five deserve mention. The first must be the establishment of historical musicology as an autonomous, scientific, and professionalized discipline; the second, the growth of a theoretically aware compositional community; the third, the introduction and dissemination of Schenker's analysis of music (with its claims to displace a more impressionistic or heuristic critique of musical works); the fourth, the availability of various analytic tools in contemporary writings on logic and mathematics; and the fifth, the advent and promise of electronic computation. Thus the composers and theorists of the time are compelled to create a discipline matching the autonomy and professionalism of musicology in its rigor, emboldened by Schenker's claims to envision fresh analytic worlds (particularly through the reconciliation of Schenker's analysis with modern music), and especially, encouraged to appropriate the authority and epistemological surety that seems within reach of contemporary philosophy.

Given this situation, it comes as no surprise that Winham's ostensible project involves the creation of a sort of metalanguage within which musical structure can come under scrutiny, and the subsequent reconstruction of the foundations of musical logic. In fact, what is most striking about Winham's work is the degree to which it is indebted to the intellectual disciplines of analytic philosophy, in particular to the work of Rudolph Carnap.[1] (Winham also appropriates elements of Alfred Tarski's semantics, Bertrand Russell's systematic logic, and Herman Weyl's work on geometric spaces. Nelson Goodman and Willard

---

[1] Of special importance is Rudolph Carnap's *Introduction to Symbolic Logic and its Applications*. Trans. William H. Meyer and John Wilkinson. (New York): Dover Publication, 1958).

Quine make brief appearances in the archive.) For example, in the undated and incomplete draft of a letter to Allen Forte [N22: 36–39], written in reference to a prospective "Princeton issue" of the *Journal of Music Theory*, Winham first confides:

> This subject is not worth writing about except in full, vigorous detail. Believe me, nobody but nobody bar myself has any idea of the complexity of this field (I had to take 18 months out to study logic and semantics and another 6 to work out how it could be applied to the musical case, and even now I can at most claim to have cleared away the major obstacles on the road to solutions).

He then sketches the contents of his proposal at length, cutting immediately to the epistemological issues that lie at the heart of music theory.

> Group I. What does music theory actually say? Does it state empirical facts? If so, are they the same kind of facts as in physical science, or is there a basic difference? What are the criteria of truth for music theory? What kind of evidence is properly invoked by it? Conversely, how can a theory about music be refuted?

> Group II. What is the relation between analysis and evaluation, i.e., can analysis demonstrate coherence or incoherence, etc., of individual works? Relatedly, (a) is theory anything more than analysis of individual works?, (b) is it even possible to analyze an incoherent work? More fundamentally still: What is coherence? What is simplicity? Complexity? etc.

The questions in the first section (accompanied by a series of casual references to outside authorities) are then given focus as a series of logical or metamathematical problems: the distinction between descriptive and analytic statements, the construction of a descriptive language within which musical relations can be examined, the definitions of musical structure and (most important) significance.[2]

> The following is a tentative order of exposition:

> 1. Introductory, on the nature of the following enterprise; specifically (1) on the concept of "explication", in which this is an essay; (2) on the language used: namely, a simplification of ordinary English, such that

---

[2]In this letter, Winham refers specifically to Leon Henkin, who worked on the structure of axiom systems for mathematics. He refers also to Herman Weyl's "Philosophie der Mathematik and Naturwissenschaft" in *Natur, Geist, Gott*, ed. A. Baeumler and M. Schröter (Munich and Berlin: R. Oldenbourg, 1927).

it can be translated into certain artificial languages for which there is a demonstrable criterion (i.e. this language is used for the central definitions and asserts; there is also a running commentary not subject to this constraint).

2. Musical analysis is stated to be the showing that certain significant relations, when confined to their exemplification in a given class of events, have a certain (logical) structure. The criteria of significance are discussed, and a proof of the necessity for such a prior criteria for significance, i.e. on the assumption that the significance of relations is a function of context, any analysis of any work A can be mechanically translated into an analysis of any other work. [This is shown to be a consequence of a theorem of Tarski; since the latter is in different terminology and in fact a different mode of speech (in Carnap's sense) from mine, it will be necessary to spend some space explaining how this theorem applies here. But this can perhaps be done with an appendix or long footnote.]

The concept of 'structure' involved is precisely defined. [Here, however, there crops up a difficulty which I have not fully resolved yet: that the above definition in the most useful form seems to be translatable only into artificial languages of a certain debatable kind, namely one having no standard model in the sense of Henkin. This difficulty also arises in the process of changing the mode of speech in applying the Tarski proof, but it is not so serious there (the reason for this is too long to explain here).]

In this section I also intend to expound at length the manner in which a recursive definition of significance can be given, and a proof that no explicit definition can be given. Probably a good way to do this from the point of view of trying to make it comprehensible will be to refer continually to the discussion of significance in geometry in Weyl's book 'Philosophy of mathematics and natural science', pointing out the similarities and differences in the cases of music and geometry. In the course of this I produce incidental explications of the concepts:

> "Significant in a given context"
>
> "Significant if . . . is significant"
>
> "Having a significant relationship to . . ."

and other notions involving significance.

An important difficulty in theory is our simple lack of knowledge of certain factors, E.G., of the structure of timbral relationships. How this affects the situation of theory in general will be discussed.

Other incidental matters cleared up along the way: (1) I give a precise distinction between analysis and mere description. Also some examples, perhaps, to show how one can determine whether writings in ordinary language are analytical or merely descriptive. (2) I show that either theory is no more than a collection of analyses, or else it must imply something about evaluation (see section 2).

He then seems to change his mind, and to redraft the previous section. (Although the previous section is not crossed out in the manuscript, there is a line break before this new material, and it returns to the same numbering and covers the same ground.)

2. I show that to the extent that an "analysis" is analytical and not merely descriptive, it can be made to directly imply something about coherence. This is so because the terms involved in defining "coherent" can be the same ones used in the assertions of analysis, namely (1) "significant" and related terms, (2) purely logico-mathematical terms such as "structure" and "relation."

In that case, the difference between theory and analysis would seem to be best construed thus: theory attempts to show that certain kinds of musical techniques or procedures are justified or unjustified in general, because of their effect on significance and hence on coherence. E.G. (trivially) that the technique of transposition is justified because it preserves all significant relations ('preserves' is among the words defined in part 1). This it can do without ever referring to specific works at all; thus in a sense it is "more than" mere analysis, or rather completely different. But nevertheless the two use the same vocabulary.

Holding this revision in abeyance for the moment (I do think it important and will return to it later), we can reconstruct to a certain extent the contents of this hypothetical article, or at least rehearse some of the applicable arguments. For example, a complex of problems surrounds the notions of the musical work, the musical score, and the notion of musical structure. Again, his unpacking of these notions has its origin in the pragmatic problem of translating the musical entity into some usable metalanguage (or at least some sort of language that would give a complete and efficient description of a piece, one amenable to analytic operations). Specifically, he begins by rejecting the simple assumption of the musical score (or musical notation in general) as itself a logically recuperable descriptive language for music [N19: 1–2].

Evidently the closest we can come to a paradigm of this is a musical score, and indeed in a sense it would be absurd to ask for a more complete description than the score, the musical work itself being definable as whatever satisfies the description given by the score. However, the "language" of scores is rather unsatisfactory in several ways. It includes elements and distinctions of problematic or no significance, such as (respectively) bar lines and differences of note-stem length; it is not always clear whether directions for physical performance or description of the intended resulting auditory affect is intended; it is vague or ambiguous in many ways; but chiefly—and this defect includes all the others—it is not the same as (or directly translatable by well known rules into) some subsystem of an ordinary verbal language (say English) for which we have more or less agreed rules of logical transformation, or alternatively into a formalized language with an interpretation. It *is*, of course, translatable into ordinary English as a whole, but this is quite an inadequate criterion, as can be seen from some parts of English which occur in scores, such as words like "Tranquilly" or phrases like "as fast as possible" (the former being objectionable as a descriptive term on the grounds of indeterminacy and nonuniformity of usage, and the latter on the ground that it presupposes a language containing modalities, where logic is far from a well-understood and agreed matter).

As with most topics in Winham's work, though, he elsewhere reconsiders this problem from a different angle, now bringing into play the relation between the musical work and the musical score [N14: 12].

By a *musical work* or *composition* we understand an abstract entity of a certain kind which may (but need not) be designated by a musical score or other linguistic or notational entity. Adopting the terminology of semantics, we may consider the musical score as a predicate-expression. Indeed a score in ordinary musical notation could obviously be translated into English (for example) if there is even any serious objection to considering that notation to simply be a part of English; and would then obviously be a predicate-expression (rather than a sentence or individual name) in that it might denote or be satisfied by a *class* of configurations (viz., the 'occurrences of' the work in question).

The configurations in question are of course sounds, in principle restricted only in that all the sounds of a configuration belong to the same aural field, although in practice theory has to confine itself to a much narrower subject-matter (such other restrictions in principle as might seems natural, such as the example that the configurations must occupy continuous segments in time, run the risk of being confronted by counter-examples—in this case "The Ring" will serve; also it ought to be mentioned here that the null class of sound-configurations must be counted as a composition in view of the fact that it has actually been composed by Mr. Cage, although we need not countenance the possibility of more than one such composition raised by its title, since we can (and do) take the view that the same sounds would satisfy any such allegedly distinct indications calling for different "amounts of silence."

And yet more intriguingly, Winham in a third passage reconceives the problem in formal terms [N28: 44–47]:

It seems obvious that the semiotical status of musical scores is that of predicates (as opposed, for example, to that of sentences). The extension of such a predicate is a class of configurations of musical events, which may be taken to be physical or phenomenal sounds, or events such as contacts between bows and strings, or various other entities, depending on the "domain" or sublanguage x such that we are considering the predicate to be a predicate-of-x.

The questions we are concerned with in this discussion are unaffected by these distinctions, so we will simply speak ambiguously of "musical events." This is not to deny that in some contexts these distinctions are of course highly relevant.

The question arises: What is the semiotic relation of a musical work to the score "of" that work?

We may quickly dispose of certain plausible suggestions:

I. The work is the extension of the score, and is denoted by it (the work is the *class* of configurations mentioned above).

This fails because *different* unperformed or unheard (etc., depending on the domain) works would all be *identical* with the null class of configurations and hence with each other.

II. The work is the intention of the score, and is designated by it (the work is a *property* of configurations of events).

This fails because logically non-equivalent scores (having, therefore, different intentions) may nevertheless be scores of the same work. This happens, for example, if two scores have the same non-null extension, i.e., are equivalent, but are nevertheless not logically equivalent in some such way as the following:

Score (a) calls for three events x, y, z to stand in the relation that x is louder than y, while y is louder than z; score (b) calls for three events x, y, z to stand in the relation that x is louder than y and y is louder than z and x is louder than z. They are not logically equivalent, because the transitivity of *louder* is not determined by logic. But they are in fact equivalent, and such a difference as this would not prevent the two scores from being scores of the same work.

One might perhaps attempt to circumvent this difficulty by claiming that score (a) is not really a "complete" score, in that it does not specify whether x is louder than z. Actually it would be easy to construct similar examples for which this device would be useless; but it is important to notice that in any case the device is illegitimate because it would not allow a score to be "purposely" unspecific, e.g., to allow various different interpretations or improvisatory passages. To require that a "complete score" determine, for every relation it mentions at all, whether this relation holds between any events for which it requires any relation to hold, would rule out the majority of actual scores.

Another attempt to circumvent the difficulty would be to suppose that the transitivity of *louder* is after all logically determined. This would require a concept of logical truth based on "meaning" rather than form, with all the attendant problems. But again, it is easy to construct other examples which would defeat such attempts. For example, certain timbres cannot belong to tones of above a certain height in pitch. But it is difficult to envisage any coherent concept of logical truth by which such facts would become logically true (at this point we are not even in full possession of a theory of sound from which they all follow).

III. The work is the class of all scores notationally similar to the given score (in some appropriate sense of 'notationally similar').

This cannot be coherently maintained in the face of the fact that (just as with verbal predicates) the same score may be a score of different works according to the language to which it is being considered to belong, even if its *syntax* is the same in both languages. For example, by a simple mapping of one such language on another, a score in ordinary notation may be mapped on the "retrograde" of the same score, both scores being well-formed expressions of both languages, but with interchange of the works of which they are scores.

IV. The work is the ordered pair of a certain language L and the class of all scores notationally similar to the given one in L.

This meets one difficulty with proposal III, but still does not provide for any sense in which scores in different languages may be scores of the same work.

One would elaborate this line further, but we can be sure that similar objections will recur to vitiate any proposal of this purely syntactical nature, because the situation is essentially analogous to the well-known syntactical indefinability of truth (for example). The relation 'score of . . .' is an irreducibly non-syntactical relation for much the same reason.

One might indeed have expected that anything so counter-intuitive as a proposal to consider the musical work to be some kind of purely notational entity would be doomed; but nevertheless such proposals have been made in all seriousness, so it is worthwhile to see just what it is that makes them untenable.

We might think here (and in a number of other similar passages) that Winham is simply making a technical point (or a sequence of technical points), but it is in this discussion that the complexities and beauties of his project become immediately apparent. Given the intellectual context of the time, Winham could have conceived his task more naively, as the simple reconstruction of analysis as a sort of algorithmic (or at least consistent) collection of rules. Yet immediately he shows us that it is not the "rules" of music that are important, or their recovery through some sort of analysis, but the conditions and presuppositions of this recovery.

In fact, this disposition is even more dramatically drawn when Winham turns to the central claim of musical analysis. He does not arrive at a definitive formulation of the relation holding between the musical score and the musical work, yet between the score and the work he locates a third entity, the musical structure. Perhaps it could be said that the work/score is entailed in some way by the particular musical structure. The notion of musical structure, though, is curiously more problematic, not because it is not amenable to a solution, but because (as indicated in his letter to Forte) a definition of "structure" is almost too conveniently at hand.

For Winham, the notion of structure can be defined in terms of a formal schema, as a subset of logicomathematical structure. An early approach to the application of a formal definition of structure is given in N19: 55–57, 144. Structure is defined as an ordered n-type $(P_1, P_2, P_3, \ldots W)$ where P is a significant property and W is the work; or it can be defined as (S, W) where S is the collection of properties preserving a one-to-one mapping of individuals on itself that preserve an arbitrary list $(P_1, P_2, P_3, \ldots P_n)$: such a structure would be said to be objective.

[A more developed, if still informal definition is contained in *37e: 1–3. Given that we can have two ordered n-tuples of relations $(A_0, A_1, A_2, \ldots A_n)$ and $(B_0, B_1, B_2, \ldots B_n)$ such that the number of arguments (not including 1) of A_n is the same as that of B_n, and given that these two n-tuples can be said to be isomorphic if and only if there is a one-to-one relation K mapping the field of one n-tuple onto another, such that if Kxy, Kx_1, y_1, . . . then $(A_nxy$ . . .$)(B_nxy)$ for each n, then the class of n-tuples isomorphic to a given n-tuple can be said to be its structure. The formal statement of this definition in the functional calculus W becomes a definition-schema; i.e., $(A_0, A_1, . . .A_n)$ and $(B_0, B_1, . . .B_m)$ are only comparable to structure within the calculus if $m = n$ and A_K and B_K are corresponding *types* for each K.]

The problem is not simply how to construe the work as an ordered n-tuple of relationships. In a similar discussion of structure [N32: 46–7] he is bothered by the dependence of this definition on cardinality. Let us say we designate a particular number of relations as significant in work W^0 and designate a like number of relations as significant in work W^1. (We remember that in N19 he had defined significant properties in terms of an arbitrary list.) There will always be some way in which these two sets of significant relations or properties can be shown to be isomorphic, and hence that the two pieces can be said to have the same "structure."

Thus the notion of structure is of no use without some definition of what constitutes a significant property. Hence [*79a: 1; I have not been able to find the examples to which Winham refers, but their sense is easily reconstructed from the context given by the passage]:

> We must next consider what could be meant, for example, by such terms as 'coherent', 'simple', etc. It seems obvious that these are to be construed as designating structural properties; hence we will represent them by names of classes of ordered n-tuples. The construction of adequate definitions of these terms is obviously a difficult and indeed profound problem; but it must be in principle solvable, if they are to have any definite meaning. As a matter of fact, there is probably a larger measure of agreement for example on what is simple, than one might immediately suppose—because discussion and argument naturally concentrate on doubtful cases. For example, probably everyone will agree that ex.1 is simpler than ex.2; and this is not difficult to "explain." We have here two sorts of relative-similarity-relation (nearness in pitch and time). In ex.1 x and y are closer in time; whereas in ex.2 the correspondence is more complicated, not expressible so simply. That this is only a vague hint at the direction of a definition is obvious; not only is it only a very special case, but what is more important, in attempting to characterize the kind of 'simplicity' involved we have moved to the syntactical mode of speech and spoken of 'simply *expressible*'. But this is clearly relative to a given terminology, and must eventually be replaced by a non-syntactical, direct characterization.

What is clear from this example is that the 'structural properties of music' are the structural properties only of certain special kinds of relations among tones, not any and all relations among them; moreover it seems obvious that the relevant relations are those which amount to the same sort of absolute or relative similarity. This, in fact, can be seen from the customary musical terminology. 'Preparation', 'associated with', 'motif', 'return', etc., are all terms having to do with similarity in a broad sense.

Hence also, though, a certain number of texts attempt heuristically to distinguish between descriptive and analytic statements about music. (The usage "analytic," in these particular writings, seems the musically local equivalent of "explanatory.") This discrimination is for Winham neither trivial or procedural, nor are its ramifications strictly metatheoretical. Indeed, he diagnoses the pathology of much of what he considers failed analysis as the unthinking conflation of the descriptive and the analytic. For example, in the draft of a letter to David Lewin, Winham criticizes a confusion between different explanations of facts with different facts to be explained in the latter's reading of Webern [*37f: 2–3]. Likewise, in an abandoned article, he attributes many of the problems of contemporary analysis to a confusion over whether disagreements pertain to description or analysis [N26: 2]. But if he finds this problem easy to diagnose in the pragmatic writings of others, he does not find (nor does he wish to find) this distinction between the descriptive and the analytic easy to draw theoretically. In fact, the informal analysis of this polarity, and its consequent implications for his formalization project (particularly in respect to constructing descriptive primitives and mapping what sort of operations would be peculiar to the musical analysis), stands at the center of his epistemic program.

In one extended (although perhaps early) work on the distinction between description and analysis [N19: 13–18], Winham unpacks a close series of existential statements:

[1] events x and y of a piece have the same pitch
[2] event x has pitch A
[3] event y has pitch A
[4] there is a pitch such that x and y have it, and that pitch is A
[5] event x has pitch A, and event y has pitch A
[6] x is similar to something in respect to having pitch A, and y is similar to something in respect to having pitch A
[7] x and y are similar in respect to being either x or y

[8] 'x and y are similar in respect to having property Q' where Q is defined as 'being x or y'

[9] x and y are similar in respect to having some property

Earlier in the notebook, Winham had sketched out the dimensional premise that any analysis must include a complete description, and hence that analysis in general must say as much or more than description [N19: 1]. Here, though, he begins from the counterpremise that analysis might be said to say less than description. On examination, we can by agreement characterize [1] as an analytic statement, and [2] and [3] as descriptive statements. [1] would seem to follow from a conjunction of [2] and [3]; and in fact it would seem to say more than [2] and [3]. Yet it does not seem to be the case that [1] says more because it is in some way logically stronger than [2] and [3] (in other words, that [2] and [3] could in some way be said to be entailed by [1]). But neither can we make the countercase that [1] says more than [2] and [3] because it is logically weaker, or because it replaces descriptive predicates with existential qualifiers. Thus, the issue of logical strength seems not to bear on the distinction between analysis and description. Of course, the analytic statement [4] seems stronger than the descriptive conjunction [5]. The difference between [4] and [5], though, seems to be a difference between statement and implication, and hence locates the distinction between analysis and description within the domain of semantics or synonymy. Although it is difficult to define with any precision what [4] states that [5] leaves unstated; perhaps [4] asserts a similarity or repetition that [5] does not. Yet [6] does likewise, seemingly without saying more than [5]. Thus, perhaps, our distinction may not rest on the assertion of a similarity. Certainly [7] would obviously assert a similarity without saying any more than [5]. Even if we were to disqualify [7] by stipulating that the predicate must be general (in other words, if we were to disallow the specificity of the phrase "similar in respect to being either x or y"), we could still rephrase [7] as [8], while still not seemingly saying more than [5]. Yet we might better think of [7] and [8] as in some way saying too much, and express them instead as [9]. It is here that we perhaps come to some understanding. Any two events, by virtue of being defined as "events," can be said logically to have something in common. Yet in analysis, statements such as [9] would be asserted with the understood proviso that only certain properties (certainly not the "Q" of [8]) could be said to count. Thus we might sufficiently define the analytic assertion as one that explicitly states that two or more things are similar, or implies (logically entails in an especially obvious matter) such. But we would also have to accept that the ascription to a statement of the status of being "analytic" seems (insomuch as it depends on external stipulation) to be one of degree.

This notion of a sort of analytic continuum, or at least the difficulty in clearly distinguishing the analytic from the descriptive (at least in the absence of a fully ramified theory) is held to in most of Winham's (perhaps subsequent) writings. In the same introduction cited earlier, he claims to have no clear or accurate idea of description [N26: 1]. But on other occasions he does reattempt such a formulation. In a letter to James Randall, he returns to the notion of a range of analyticity (while holding that there is some "degree-zero" of pure description). Yet here he ventures more. He speculates that the explanatory power of a statement may derive not from either simplicity or formal strength, but rather from the ratio of strength to simplicity [*48: 1–3]. In the same notebook from which we drew Winham's extended discussion, he later speculates that the difference between analysis and description could be said to be "ultra-intentional," and hence that equivalent assertions are not necessarily both or neither analytic, and moreover that the complete description of a totally-determined work (in which category he would include classical tonal music) implies an analysis (although the reverse is not the case) [N19: 139]. And yet later in the same notebook he wonders whether description, like analysis, presumes the notion of "same in every musical respect."

Finally, though, in what is most likely a later work, Winham claims to have dissolved this problem [*37a: 2–7; Pt. 2, Ex. I]. He asserts that the purely descriptive statement is one that cannot be rephrased as an analytic statement, and moreover that the latter is such that it cannot be deduced from the former. In other words, descriptiveness depends on intent, and presumes a lack of entailment. But more interestingly, he lets his argument take a pragmatic turn. He asserts that the difficulty in discriminating between analytic and descriptive statements arises because we tend to falsely believe that descriptive statements can be reworded as analytic statements that are logically equivalent or weaker. But any such rewording will almost inevitably introduce certain unacknowledged claims through the connotation of new words. He asks that we consider three statements:

[1] Work W begins with middle C.

[2] Work W ends with middle C.

[3] Work W begins and ends with the same pitch.

Statements [1] and [2] would together seem to imply [3], yet the reverse is not the case, so [3] seems logically weaker. But [3] supposes the *a priori* significance of the relation "beginnings and endings" and of the relation "same in pitch." Thus [3] implies covertly two qualitative classes that have the same extension of events in work W. Thus [3] is stronger in that it makes claims as to the significance of some properties of relationships among musical events as opposed to other properties. And thus, at least one such predicate must be taken as an ultimate primitive in a formalized system, and certain statements that satisfy if taken as axioms (in addition to the list of descriptive statements of the work).

The Phenomenal Construction of the Musical Subject

A simple attack on the problem of the analyticity of various statements, while enforcing a sort of discursive rigor, promises though no solution to the question of musical significance. Nor, of course, does it engage the question of what sort of calculus (syntactic or semiotic) is to give us the most accurate insight into the workings of music. Winham, instead, engages this question in a different manner.

The material quoted in the previous section has already provided us with some clues as to the nature of this engagement. We first recall the revision of his letter to Forte.

> 2. I show that to the extent that an "analysis" is analytical and not merely descriptive, it can be made to directly imply something about coherence. This is so because the terms involved in defining "coherent" can be the same ones used in the assertions of analysis, namely (1) "significant" and related terms, (2) purely logico-mathematical terms such as "structure" and "relation."
>
> In that case, the difference between theory and analysis would seem to be best construed thus: theory attempts to show that certain kinds of musical techniques or procedures are justified or unjustified in general, because of their effect on significance and hence on coherence. E.G. (trivially) that the technique of transposition is justified because it preserves all significant relations ('preserves' is among the words defined in part 1). This it can do without ever referring to specific works at all; thus in a sense it is "more than" mere analysis, or rather completely different. But nevertheless the two use the same vocabulary.

This passage reveals that concealed beneath Winham's ostensible project (the construction of a language and logic within which to speak of music) lies a more interesting agenda. Given the situation, the speculative theorists of the time could not but preoccupy themselves with the very nature and claims of music theory, and particularly with its relation to the analysis of concrete works, and it is in this relation, and the varying ways in which it can be conceived, that Winham looks to define musical significance. Three particular stances are found in Winham's work, each of which presumes a different relation between music theory and musical analysis. The first is the most familiar, predicated on the notion of theory as a generalization of what might be thought of as covering laws from a body of analytic observations of a defined canon of musical texts. (Schenker's theory of tonal music, for example, ostensibly assumes this stance.) The second arises from theory's reflection on this process of generalization from analytic observation, and turns on its interrogation of its own precision, coherence, and completeness, thus correcting imprecisions, incoherences, and incomplete formulations and gaining access to new musical insights and intuitions. (In a way, Winham's attempt at some sort of rationalized metalanguage reflects just this sort of stance.) The third is more subtle and not easily distinguished from the second. Theory, in a sense, separates itself from analysis and thus interrogates itself, questioning its own status and assumptions as a discipline.

All three of these stances complement an ongoing analytic practice in Winham's writings. The first informs an attempt to generate new theories of consonance, or chord stability, of prolongation and the like. The second informs a critique of the mechanics of analysis, an attempt to precisely define such notions as "levels" and "tonal operations." But the third of these, which in a very real way is the result of Winham's inability to formulate a convincing semiotic of music, is the most interesting. To come at the question of what constitutes a significant relation in the musical text, he effectively postulates two sorts of musical significance, the first of which is reconstructable in some epistemologically transparent manner, and the second of which is contingent. The first falls within an autonomous domain of theory, the second within the domain of analysis (or the theory of analysis). This seems a simple, if not anachronistic, conceptual opposition. But as developed by Winham, it becomes something subtle and striking, and richly reworks the relation between theory and analysis. Rather than arguing theory as a collection of covering laws, as a practice strictly dependent on observation or analysis, or arguing an analysis contingent on the choice of theory (its effectiveness contingent on the rationalization of that theory), Winham arrives at a very delicate and balanced structure embracing theory and analysis, one in which the claims of each are circumscribed, but one in which the possibilities of each become apparent and a defined notion of musical structure can come into being.

Yet another clue to this different agenda is found in a line of reasoning that Winham perhaps too readily dismisses in a passage quoted earlier.

> Another attempt to circumvent the difficulty would be to suppose that the transitivity of *louder* is after all logically determined. This would require a concept of logical truth based on "meaning" rather than form, with all the attendant problems. But again, it is easy to construct other examples which would defeat such attempts. For example, certain timbres cannot belong to tones of above a certain height in pitch. But it is difficult to envisage any coherent concept of logical truth by which such facts would become logically true (at this point we are not even in full possession of a theory of sound from which they all follow).

The key to the notion of musical significance, to an autonomous theoretical domain, and hence finally to a theory of analysis or musical structure, lies in the very notion that a quality such as loudness is transitive, or in other words, it in itself is amenable to an analysis, and thus that a theory of sound is possible.

Of course, this notion of a theory of sound demands immediate qualification. Its subject must be the musical phenomenon as distinguished not only from notations but also from both physical sound and sense-data [N19: 31–34; Pt. 2, Ex. II]. (This last position is perhaps ruled out *a priori* by the construal of the musical work as an intentional event [N32: 14].) In other words, the subject of analysis could be the tone, a phenomenal event, but could not be the sound wave, a physical event, or, in contrast, some subjective observational report.

That the domain of musical phenomena is subject to analysis is easily demonstrated. For example, the temporality of tonal music is governed by a phenomenal asymmetry that differs uniquely from any asymmetry of tonal pitch relations. Several portions of the archive [*1f, *25b, N1, N2] grasp at this phenomenon. I pick one brief exposition [*25b] of this idea:

> In tonality, the preferred order of dependent and independent elements is for the former to precede the latter; or to put it another way, the abstract relation of dependence is concretely expressed or articulated by that of precedence rather than its converse.
>
> This relation between relations is somewhat analogous to the expression of dependence within simultaneities by aboveness, but there is an important difference. This vertical relation, though perhaps

grounded in the same psychological factor which leads us to assign the names 'up' and 'down' to the pitch-directions, may seem to be a free choice between possibilities; or at least, if it is not, there is no clearly known reason why it should not be so. In the case of the temporal relation, however, there are good grounds for supposing that we have no choice in the matter. There is no converse to memory, and any analysis of a piece which fails to take this fact into account must be incomplete.

This may be done as follows: every piece is regarded as a collection of sets of events, which constitute a linear order with respect to inclusion as the generating relation. The smallest set consists of the beginning events, etc. It is then evident the retrograde of the same piece (even if physically possible) has a different structure with respect to temporal order. The relation of being earlier is mapped on that of being later (and conversely) only for the largest set, in general.

For example, the temporally ordered set of occurrences

$$(AABA)$$

gives rise, by virtue of memory, to the (unordered) set of temporally ordered sets

$$[(A), (AA), (AAB), (AABA)]$$

while the temporally ordered set of occurrences

$$(ABAA)$$

gives, by virtue of memory, to the set

$$[(A), (AB), (ABA), (ABAA)].$$

The analysis of these two 'pieces' then differs in such ways as the following: in the first the unique element B appears in just half of the sets; in the second, it appears in three out of four.

This method may thus be used to explain the hitherto mysterious difference in (felt) structure between configurations and their retrogrades in general. But our immediate problem is to apply it to the case of dependency relations such as those of tonal music.

This is not difficult. Inclusion is the set-structural analog of the basic explanatory relation of material implication. For example, in the simplest case of just two elements A and B in that temporal order, we have the total

$$[(A), (AB)]$$

The A may be explained in terms of its dependence on B, if it does depend on B. But the B as such does not require such explanation, as there is no B heard in isolation, i.e., conversely, this temporal order of A and B is functionless if B depends on A, and the A itself remains unexplained in terms of the whole.

But in addition, it may be observed that in tonality dependence relations are often associated with other kinds of inclusion (E.G., the root of the V triad is included in the I triad). In these cases this kind of inclusion, when associated with subsequence in time, is brought into parallelism with what we may call 'memorative inclusion'.

Since inclusion and dependence are almost the same concept, this association is no surprise.

The phenomenal event occupies a sort of tangibly psychological but intersubjective middle ground between notational abstraction, physical event, and sense-data. Also, though, Winham specifies that this phenomenological domain exists in a middle ground between logicomathematical and empirical domains (the latter represented musically by psychoacoustics). This makes his definition of field much more elusive. Early on, he accepts that the complexity of logical statements might in some way be a criteria for inclusion into analysis, yet rejects any psychoacoustic standard for such inclusion (a standard critique phrased in the form "such and such a statement of logical relations is too complex to be heard") [N19: 6]. Yet he immediately grants that empirical evidence does come into play in relation to properties such as "earlier-than" and "later-than" [N19: 9]. In another manuscript [N37: 5], he specifies that the truth-criteria for axioms resides ultimately in psychoacoustics (denying the free choice of axioms), defines a sufficient description of a work in which statements need not be independent or relevant, but must be based on laws of sound phenomena, and specifies that analytic statements can only be deduced from axioms and sufficient descriptions together. A third manuscript mandates that primitive predicates designate directly evident properties or relations of phenomena [N32: 12], that such observational primitives could include "higher-in-pitch" or "earlier" or "louder" or "oboe" [N32: 34], that "laws of sound" (such as the specification that the relation "higher-in-pitch" is transitive, asymmetric, and irreflexive) govern these predicates, and that all empirical questions about these laws be ultimately decided by psychoacoustics [N32: 35].

But it is also in this phenomenal domain that questions can be answered with some surety. In effect, Winham dissolves (or places in suspension) the whole semiotic tangle of work/score, structure/significance, and analysis/description by declaring such questions premature. In fact, the description of a musical event, or the selection of criteria for musical significance, or even the identification of the musical piece is impossible without an understanding of the domain of musical phenomenology, which stands anterior to this semiotics.

The Axiomatic Construction of Phenomena

This turn away from the structure (as such) of the musical work itself to the structure of musical phenomena (in general) is the key move in Winham's strategy, for unlike the supposed structure of the work, the structure of musical phenomena is more convenient to analysis. It is here that Winham can to more profit avail himself of the tools of the analytic philosopher. Specifically, he draws on the work of Rudolph Carnap, reconstructing the laws of musical phenomena within axiomatic systems. (Carnap speaks of *P-laws* whose truth-value stands outside of that of logical laws: Winham uses this locution once [N32: 78–82], but speculates elsewhere that this methodology might allow, in principle, a sufficient description of the work in which statements need not be logically true but may be phenomenally true; although it does not rule out logically true statements [N32: 34]).[3]

To illustrate, we take a simple axiomatic phenomenology of pitch [*79b; recapitulated and expanded in *79d]. Most important, we note that what makes this analysis more available than Winham's semiotic analysis is the ability to specify *a priori* what constitutes a significant relation, and hence what constitutes (at this level) "musical structure." The particular properties of relations in this system are those given by Carnap.[4] A relation is symmetrical if it is identical with its converse: the relation "contemporaneous" is symmetrical; "brother" is nonsymmetrical; and "father" is asymmetrical. Two events that within their field are always fulfilled are reflexive: "contemporaneous" is reflexive; "teacher" is nonreflexive; and "father" is irreflexive. A relation is transitive if it holds for the next member of a class but one: "ancestor" is transitive; "friend" is nontransitive; and "father" is intransitive. [Insomuch as both passages (particularly *79d) give out this system in a series of mostly uninterpreted formulae, I will supply a paraphrase and interpretation.]

---

[3]See, for example, Rudolph Carnap, *The Logical Syntax of Language*. Trans Amethe Smeaton (London: Routledge & Kegan Paul, 1959), 315–322.

[4] Rudolph Carnap, *Introduction to Symbolic Logic and its Applications*, 119–120.

Winham first stipulates a primitive description "lower in pitch," and specifies in his first axiom that this relation is transitive and irreflexive. (We might read this as "if there is an x which is lower than a y, there is a z which is lower than both x and y; and if there is an x lower than y, then y cannot be lower than x)."

A1. $(L^2 \subset L) \bullet (L \subset {\sim}I)$

He then defines the (intransitive) quality "pitch-unordered" where some x (which may be a single pitch event or a chord or an indefinite pitch) is neither entirely higher (as indicated by the superscript "-1") or entirely lower than some y.

D1. $PU = (L \downarrow L^{-1})$

Next we are given a two-place definition of a quality designated "definite pitch." (I read this as "x is a definite pitch if for a y and for a z, if x and y are pitch-unordered, and x and z are pitch-unordered, then y and z are pitch-unordered.")

D2. $DPx \equiv (y)(z)(PUxy \bullet PUxz \supset PUyz)$

From here, two events, if both are pitch-unordered and both are definite pitches, can be defined as "same-pitch."

D3. $SPpxy \equiv (PUxy \bullet DPx \bullet DPy)$

This in turn leads to two theorems, the first of which designates *pitch-unordered* as reflexive and symmetrical (read as "x is pitch-unordered to itself, and if x is pitch-unordered to y, y is pitch-unordered to x": this relation is not, though, transitive), and the second of which (read as "if x is same-pitch to y, and y is same-pitch to z, x is same-pitch to z") designates *same-pitch* as transitive. (It is of course reflexive and symmetrical.)

T1. $(I \subset PU) \bullet (PU \subset PU^{-1})$

T2. $SP^2 \subset SP$

Winham then puts forward three more definitions and five theorems (these are found only in [*79d]). Any x and y are "pitch-similar" if any z pitch-unordered to x is pitch-unordered to y.

D4. $PSxy \equiv PU\,(z,x) \subset PU(z,y)$

A "pitch-quality" is a class having a member that is pitch-similar to every member and to no nonmember. (I read this as "if a class of events F has a pitch-quality when for some x, which is a member of F, and a y, if y is a member of F, then x and y are pitch-similar.")

D5. $PQ(F) \equiv (\exists x)(Fx \bullet (y)(Fy \equiv PSxy))$

A "definite-pitch-quality" is a pitch-quality containing a definite pitch.

D6. $DPQ(F) \equiv (PQ(F) \bullet (\exists F \bullet DP))$

Pitch-similarity is transitive and symmetrical.

T3. $(Ps \subset PS^{-1}) \bullet (PS^2 \subset PS)$

If an event x and an event y are pitch-similar, either both or neither are definite pitches.

T4. $(x)(y)$ $(PSxy \supset (DP \equiv DPy))$

If an event x and an event y are pitch-similar, and x is a definite pitch, then x and y are the same pitch.

T5. $(x)(y)(PSxy \bullet DPx \supset SPxy)$

Any two members of a pitch-quality class stand in the relation of pitch-similarity.

T6. $(F)(x)(y)(PQ\,(F) \bullet Fx \bullet Fy \supset PSxy)$

Any two members of a definite-pitch-quality class have the relation of being the same pitch.

T7. $(F)(x)(y)(DPQ(F) \bullet Fx \bullet Fy \supset SPxy)$

From this point, several different paths are possible in regard to fixing or assigning pitches. Winham sketches three options [*79d: 7]. In the first ("L_1"), the universe is limited to definite pitches of the standard scale. Introducing the relation "SL" (semitone lower) as a primitive gives rise to the axiom that the relation is necessarily transitive:

$(SL^{>0} \downarrow SL^{-1>0})$

With the addition of a second primitive "MC" (middle C), the universe of pitches can be defined thus

$MC\#x \equiv (MC(-) \subset SL(-,x))$

and complemented by a second axiom that establishes MC as a pitch-quality. [This definition provides that for any event specified as middle C ("MC" being a convention rather than "x = 256 c.p.s.") there stands a pitch that is a semitone higher: this in itself constructs the chromatic scale. The axiom provides that two such events must either be equal in pitch or stand some multiple of semitones apart.]

$$MCx \bullet MCy \supset (SL^{>0} \downarrow SL^{-1>0})$$

A second universe ("L_2") would allow nonpitches, defining definite pitch ("DP") through the introduction of a primitive "L" ("lower"). [An event is a definite pitch if it is higher or lower than two other events respectively, and these two other events are higher or lower in relation to each other: this formula allows events of indefinite pitch in that two tones may be unordered when defined in terms of an indefinite pitch.]

$$DPx \equiv (y)(z)(L \downarrow L^{-1})xy \bullet (L \downarrow L^{-1})xz \supset (L \downarrow L^{-1})yz$$

A third universe ("L_3"), designed specifically for the tonal system, might allow two differing semitones, the scale-step and the chromatic alteration.

In sum, from the single primitive "lower-in-pitch" Winham develops a rich and unfamiliar vocabulary for speaking of pitch events. Particularly and intriguingly unsettling is his location of "definite pitch" not as a primitive but rather as one among several sorts of pitch events, and also (in his description of "pitch-quality" and "definite-pitch-quality") of the notion of classes to handle the recurrence of similar events in the course of a passage: in the best of analytic traditions, he opens a world of relations anterior to what we would customarily regard as the basic relations of music theory and musical notation.

What is also striking, though, is that Winham's exposition again engages a phenomenal rather than a physical world. His argument does not require a physical description of, let us say, two events that are "pitch-unordered" to each other. But neither is this, as of yet, a logical calculus, yielding formulae that we can assert are in substance logically true: his definition of, let us again say, the relation "pitch-unordered" does not logically entail the theorem that this relation is reflexive and symmetrical. Rather, it exposes a phenomenal truth anterior to logical truth. (This becomes particularly apparent when he subsequently introduces "semitone" and "middle-C" into his system as primitives. As noted, "middle-C" is not defined physically but phenomenally, and thus constitutes only an unspecified reference point against which can be gauged other such points, and the notion of "semitone," as is particularly apparent in Winham's thoughts about a language for tonal music, is likewise not defined physically but phenomenally.)

Of course the phenomenal laws of pitch are rather easily available to inspection (insomuch as they have been the subject of study for many hundreds of years). By contrast, the phenomenal laws that govern other qualia, such as time, attack, dynamic, or color, are (to differing degrees) less immediately given to our reflection. With the limited exception of temporality, Winham does not develop the same sort of argument for any of these qualia that he develops for pitch, yet he does give significant attention to the sort of phenomenal suppositions that would be necessary to develop such arguments. For time, he notes that although one might look to define for some piece the minimal temporal length allowable to individuals from the highest common factor of durations between changes, and thus speak of time in some way comparable to the way in which one speaks of scaled pitch, perceptual time does not constitute such a uniform structure, and hence one must speak of proportions: he also notes that temporal relations are more complex than pitch relations [*79e: 3–4]. For attack, he notes the problem of distinguishing, let us say, two simultaneous attacks from a pitch held in one instrument and attacked in another [*79g]; notes the problem of comparing attacks of different timbres and dynamics; and shows a certain unease with the notion of attack as an abbreviation for the complex conditions governing the initiation of a tone [*79n: 34].

The phenomenal laws governing dynamics and color (or timbre) are if anything less immediately given. Speaking of dynamics, Winham notes that any system must make a distinction between silence and nonexistence. Silence is a dynamic value if it is the null class of a dynamic progression [*79c: 1], and insomuch as time-quality is easily coinstantiated with silence, it would not seem unreasonable to likewise coinstantiate pitch and color with silence (particularly in that many pieces seem to end sometime after their last sounded pitch) [*79e: 1–2]. And again, Winham notes the association of silence with the *pianissimo* dynamic [*79n: 6]. Further, he rejects the numerical scaling of dynamics as phenomenally unrealistic [*79c], but does arrive at the characterization of the dynamic relation as transitive, asymmetrical, and connected [*79n: 6].

Speaking of color [exclusively in *79u, 3–6; Pt. 2, III], Winham seems to work on grounds that are more familiar phenomenally through the received precepts of orchestration. He begins with the notion of primitive descriptions such as *violin, cello, oboe* and *bassoon*. He then notes, though, that one must include such terms as *string* or *woodwind*, terms that are problematic insomuch as one must decide whether they denominate classes or individuals. He thus rejects such obvious primitives as "violin," turning instead to a primitive constitution of similarity: if two notes are sounded on the same instrument, let us say "VLN," they would have a similarity value of C^0, if "STR," C^1, if VLN and OB, C^2. He then speculates further on the plausibility of a four-dimensional similarity array determined by color, brightness, clarity, and mixture. Further, though, he notes that one would still have to deal with phenomenally unique events such as the "emergent" colors resulting from the mixture of a violin and a clarinet.

In sum, the phenomenal domains of time, attack, dynamic, and color should manifest their own laws, yet, as Winham discovers, these laws are for a number of reasons not so easily recovered. In part, the problem is one of simplicity. Winham's efforts to recover these laws are closely bound to his selection of descriptive primitives, and hence governed by a preference for axiomatic economy: to speak of but one case, he is very uncomfortable with his tentative notion of a four-dimensional descriptive matrix for color. Likewise, a second problem in deriving phenomenal laws is connectivity. Winham is aware of the difficulties attending the separation of phenomenal domains: in fact, in one of his most interesting passages, he most strikingly turns this difficulty into a strength by speculating on the plausibility of defining octave-equivalence not as a pitch relation but rather as a color relation [*79u].

The Phenomenal Structure of Harmonic Events

Returning to the domain of pitch, we remember that Winham's simplest possible language ("L_1") added the axiom "semitone lower" to his previous set of propositions with the aim of constructing the world of definite pitches. ("L_2," we remember, expanded this universe to include nonpitches; "L_3" proposed the introduction of two different primitives as semitones to lay a foundation for an explanation of the difference between scale-step semitones and chromatic alterations in tonal music.) We gain some sense of the possible extensions of L_1 by looking at a partially or potentially axiomatic system of tonal pitch relations put forward by Winham's colleague James K. Randall in the first part of a projected book entitled *Tonality* (a draft of which is contained in the Winham archive).

Although Randall does deduce definitions and even quasi-theorems from his axioms, we might speak of his expositions simply as a propositional sequence. (This distinction will take on some importance later.) Taking the pitch (or, more precisely, specific pitch such as could be designated by A = 440 c.p.s.) as his initial uninterpreted primitive element, Randall

    1) stipulates the half-step (as a primitive relation); defines (in terms of his two primitives) the relations "identical pitch," and "distinct pitch"; stipulates the notion of a set of distinct

pitches; and defines the relations "next higher" and "next lower" holding among a collection of distinct pitches each of which manifests a semitone relation with two other pitches.

2) defines octave-equivalence (in terms of places in a complete set of distinct pitches) and extends these definitions of relations to hold between classes of pitches (pitch-classes) defined by octave-equivalence.

3) defines the collection of distinct pitch-classes and stipulates subcollections and cardinal classes of subcollections (dyad, trichord).

4) defines the transposition of subcollections and the notion of distinct transpositions (in which pitch-class does not coincide for all elements of the subcollection and its transposition); defines the common tone holding between subcollections and their transpositions; and stipulates a common tone index.

5) defines ordered sets (or subcollections).

6) defines the chromatic interval, its complement in relation to the octave, the interval class, its complement, and the "normal form" denomination of subcollections of pitch-classes.

7) defines adjacency and nonadjacency within ordered subcollections, the determinacy or indeterminacy of an adjacency with respect to a specific collection, and a property holding within certain collections where every interval is either an adjacency or nonadjacency and is thereby strongly determinate.

8) stipulates a special set of collections (modeled by the pitch-class collection $[0, 2, 4, 6, 7, 9, 11]$) that in normal form manifests every interval class (all of which are strongly determined), has twelve distinct transpositions; and manifests every possible common tone index between at least one pair of transpositions.

9) defines this collection as a "chain" (in that every place is generated by a single interval, i.e., $[0, 7, 2, 9, 4, 11, 6]$) and specifies a convention whereby any chain of interval 7 is to be specified by its initial pitch and the size of the collection.

10) defines the trichord as the maximal subcollection of such a chain not containing any adjacencies; distinguishes three classes of trichords (major, minor, diminished); demonstrates how the respective sets of all possible major or minor trichords within a given chain in normal form exhaust the pitch content

of that chain; and thus stipulates that each such trichord can be seen as a trichordal generator of the chain.

11) demonstrates how a given chain shares the highest common tone index (6) with two nonidentical chains whose initial pitch-classes are five and seven semitones above; demonstrates how a given chain and its two most nearly related chains share one major and one minor trichord; and designates these trichords as the tonic major and the tonic minor.

12) defines scalar ordering in terms of pairs of consequent places adjacent in ordering in normal form.

13) shows how within a given chain three scalar orderings (partial scales) are bounded (and only bounded) by pitch-classes of the tonic major (or tonic minor); demonstrates how these three scalar orderings show a strong bias (i.e., smaller intervals of adjacency) toward one-pitch class of the tonic-major trichord (or tonic-minor trichord) and a weaker bias toward a second pitch-class of the tonic-major (or tonic-minor) scalar tetrachord; and terms the first the biased tonic-major (or -minor) pitch-class and the second the unbiased tonic-major (or -minor) pitch-class. [For example, given the tonic trichord of a chain, and given also the scalar ordering of that chain, there exist three scalar orderings in which the tonic trichord is represented in and only in the first and last places (in other words, for the chain constructed on F, the diatonic scale segments between C and E, E and G, and G and C). All possible ordered subsets—dyads and trichords—of these segments are either biased or unbiased toward pitches of the tonic trichord depending on their placement (or nonplacement) of the minimal interval of adjacency (the semitone). Hence the chain, taken in its tonic-major form, is biased toward one pitch-class (in our example, C), neutral toward another (E), and unbiased toward the third (G). Comparably, the same chain taken in its tonic-minor form is biased toward one pitch-class (E), neutral toward another (C), and unbiased toward a third (A).]

14) generates from this four provisional pitch systems that fall into two classes, the first of which comprises the major system (which is biased) and the inverted mixolydian system (unbiased), the second the inverted phrygian system (biased) and the minor system (unbiased), and shows how the first and fourth systems (together the tonal system) and the second and third systems are respectively compatible with respect to root relations.

This quick review does not do justice to Randall's rather elegant argument, yet it enables us to make certain points. Most important, Randall conceives tonality in terms of a field (whose elements are definite pitches) possessing certain structures (the metric provided by the absolute interval of the semitone, and the further metric of the octave) within which unfolds a set-theoretical mechanics predicated on the specification of subcollections or sets of elements from the field, the specification of relations between sets (isomorphism, intersection), the representation of sets in a usable manner (normal form), the internal structure of sets (adjacency and nonadjacency within ordered normal form representation), and the properties of a bounded collection specific to tonality (generation of the collection by interval-class chain, perfect distinction between adjacency and nonadjacency, exhaustion of pitch content by transpositions of trichords of nonadjacency, hierarchization of elements within the collection, etc.). The benefits of this argument are obvious. Pragmatically, it codifies many of the insights about the tonality that had become common currency (such as the unique multiplicity of interval class in the tonal collection). Ideologically, it repictures tonality as a system among a world of possible systems (albeit one that exploits certain remarkable properties of the pitch world). As a corollary to this last point, it distinguishes itself from received theory by its nonintroduction of essentialist definitions (or possible definitions) of certain terms (such as *consonant, scale*, etc.) and even manages to refract the major/minor distinction of received theory in the doubled symmetry of the biased and unbiased systems.

We might think of Randall's argument as a particularly developed exemplar of a standard model of tonality current in music theory circles of the time. On certain of these points, Winham thinks of himself as being in agreement with Randall. (Particular discussions of Randall's system are found in *2h, N1, N14, N18, N20, and N33.) His own conception of tonality, though, leads him in a strikingly different direction.

A sense of this direction comes through in the axiomatic argument of pitch presented earlier. Winham is extremely careful about what he will and what he will not assert. For instance, in defining the relation "pitch-unordered," he works solely from the axiomatic relation "lower-than." His argument, though, makes no claims as to what sort of events can be pitch-unordered. In fact, be they specific pitches, complexes of specific pitches, frequency bands, or whatever, they are under this definition indistinguishable. Even the stipulation of definite pitch (i.e., the condition that holds when one event is pitch-unordered to two other events, and the two other events are pitch-unordered to each other) does not mandate an event of the order $A = 440$ c.p.s. but only an event that is by comparison with other events bounded and stable. In fact, I believe that it is only with the definition of "definite-pitch-quality" that we must truly understand the events to which Winham's system applies as equivalent to "pitches" in the real world (or in Randall's sense).

Each definition, though, refers to a pitch event. (The theorems, of course, refer to the logical structure of these relations.) Each, in Winham's terms, is translatable into an analytic statement about given phenomena. We might go so far as to think of this analysis as phenomenological: it uncovers layers of musical intuitions. (I use this term guardedly, aware of its connotations. Certainly I would not equate Winham's axiology with the reductive disciplines of continental phenomenology.) Yet the application of the axiomatic method to musical events differs from its application to, let us say, geometry or biological systems: in the case of the former it is applied to the perception of events, in the case of the latter to empirically given facts. Thus, the definition of phenomenal relations in Winham's system is of more importance than the explication of the logical structure of these relations in associated theorems. (As we shall see, Winham's axiomatic system can survive as a sequence of just definitions.) In this sense, little in Randall's sequence of propositions is phenomenological. It is accurate and even interesting to define a triad as the maximal subcollection of non-adjacent members within an ordered interval-7 chain in normal form, which has the property that in three transpositions it exhausts the pitch content of that chain-collection. Yet, this definition maps a system rather than a perception.

Thus, Winham's examination of the pitch matrix of tonal phenomena (or harmonic events) is necessarily the reconstruction of a phenomenological logic. As sympathetic as he is to the notion of tonality as one system among any number of musical systems, he must accept the perception of such qualities as consonance as having some phenomenal reality. (Interestingly, given his ideology, Winham in one place asserts that the phenomenology of tonality applies also to atonal works, the difference being that in the latter the phenomenal relations are for the most part unexploited or incoherent. This does not, however, invalidate the music.)

Winham comments directly on this subject. For one thing, he is suspicious of the reification of discrete pitch relations that is an uninterrogated assumption of the "standard theory." We read [N37: 28]:

> The borderline, indeed, between individual tone and certain 'chords' is not sharp—as might be expected from the very small variation in their physical correlates in some cases. It must be granted at once that

theory is by no means master of this complex situation. No general criterion determining even what physical sounds will be resolved by the ear into single tones is known; it may well vary so greatly between different ears that it would be of no particular use for musical purposes anyway—not to mention the even more damaging result bound to be produced by different performances. (This last point may be obsoleted by the development of electronic music). Over the last fifty years, it seems that the tendency of music has been to definitely separate the relations of individual tones of definite, unique pitch from other relations of sounds. The former are organized ever more precisely and are able to account for the pitch-organization of the music ever more completely; the latter are relegated to the wholly secondary sphere habited, for example, by timbral organization (about which we know almost nothing). Consequently, simultaneity of tones is in this music hardly more than their temporal identity; or, to put it another way, the chord is considered simply as the conjunction of its constituent tones.

This is not to infer that he rejects the notion of specific pitch. Rather, he defines specific pitch in terms of the physically given relations of the overtone system. But specific pitch thus cannot come into being logically without carrying with them the collection of relations embodied in the overtone series.

Further arguments against the "Randall model" (as such) are given explicitly in the following text:

Several attempts have been made to found the theory of tonality on the basis of facts concerning only the relation of *octave-equivalence* and *intervallic size* alone, disregarding *tone-overtone* relations. A sufficient motivation for such attempts is given by two considerations: In the first place the former facts are quite clear, well understood, and at least in the simplest cases, obvious, whereas the latter are relatively complicated and obscure. Secondly, it is easy to show that the former are relevant, whereas the relevance of the latter has recently been made doubtful by several developments, among which are the prevalence of new musical systems which disregard them (especially the twelve-tone system) and the discovery of new analytical methods, capable of showing interrelation between many factors in music formerly thought to be entirely separate.

Yet it turns out that we can show the insufficiency of a basis limited to facts concerning the former two relations by the same kind of arguments as those by which we show their relevance; and so, if we are determined to avoid invoking overtone relations in any way, we end by having to make a number of further assumptions about different aspects of tonality. These further assumptions, however, can all be derived from certain quite weak assumptions concerning the tone-overtone relations, constituting only the least doubtful and obscure part of what has been generally asserted in this area, or rather: constituting a simplification and clarification of even that part.

To show the relations of (1) octave-equivalence and (2) intervallic size, let us consider the transformations of one musical configuration into another which could be considered structure-preserving if these relations, respectively, are not counted as part of what needs to be preserved.

The essential point about (1) is that it sets an absolute standard of size. If (1) is irrelevant, then the analysis of any configuration C^1, resulting from a configuration C by multiplying all intervals by some constant, should be the same as that of C.

In the case of (2), the results are even more absurd; if this were irrelevant, we should have as a structure-preserving transformations such operations as the distortion of the pitch range such that every interval C–D-flat is mapped on an interval C–F-sharp, while the complement D-flat–C is squeezed into the remaining half octave. And even this assumes that at least the relations of height-order are preserved, because of an assumption of relevance of a *betweenness* relation (such an assumption is not necessary if (2) is invoked, for we can define betweenness as follows: the pitch X is between the pitches Y and Z if and only if X and Z are different pitches and the intervals (X,Y) and (Y,Z) are both smaller than (X,Z)).

But even given both (1) and (2), we still have as structure-preserving transformations the operations of transposition and of total-inversion. Transposition raises no difficulty because it is generally admitted to actually be structure-preserving; in the case of inversion, however, it seems extremely doubtful that it should be so considered. Even if we cannot give any reason why we should not do so, we can hardly accept the total-inversion of some classical composition as being analytically indistinguishable from the original; and it would then appear as a historical oddity that no compositions 'in the inverted tonal system' have been written. This, then, is the first point at which an extra assumption would be necessary.

The second point arises out of the confinement of tonality to a gamut of just twelve pitch-classes. It is easy enough to find some property of this gamut having some particular relevance to tonality; but it is not at all easy to show that no other equal division of the octave would have equally relevant properties.

It may be thought that this is not a very serious problem, in that to provide a basis for the usual tonal system is not to assert that there could not be other similar systems based on the other gamuts; and the historical fact that these have never been used is subject to simple enough explanation, thus differing completely from the other historical 'oddity' mentioned above. However, the matter is not so simple; for in those theories which ignore the tone-overtone relations, some special significances of particular intervals (e.g., that the fifth is the primary harmonic interval) have to be explained in terms of their structural relationship to the gamut (e.g., by observing certain consequences of the fact that 7 is prime to 12). Thus the structure of the gamut itself is an important assumption in those theories; and while, for reasons given above, there is no particular objection to such an assumption, the fact remains that it is one, and that it would be a merit of a theory to make it unnecessary.

A third difficulty arises out of the possibility of the operation of inversion in the sense of *complementation of the intervallic distances with respect to the octave* (as opposed to total inversion). This operation is clearly not structure-preserving in general, since it affects the relative-minimal-sizes of the different interval-classes. However, no satisfactory explanation has been given of how that difference is related to the differences of treatment of complementary intervals in tonal music. (As an example of an unsatisfactory explanation, consider the view according to which the difference of consonance between the fifth and fourth derives from the fact that the fifth is obtainable directly from the superimposition of minimal diatonic nonadjacencies, whereas the fourth has to be obtained by a more complex process in that superimposition plus complementation is necessary; this view is unsatisfactory because if degree of consonance is to be thus identified with simplicity of derivation from superimposition of thirds and complementation, it would follow that the *third is more consonant than the fifth*; and thus the consequences of this principle turn out to contradict part of just what it was presumably supposed to explain. Indeed, it seems prima facie at least very unlikely that relative minimal-size of the *consonances* and their complements has any particular significance, since the relative size of octave-*equivalent* consonances certainly does not.)

A fourth difficulty is curiously enough one that has often been supposed to be a difficulty with theories which do assume something about overtones—namely, the peculiarities of the minor mode. It is obvious that there is a general difference between the treatment of the major and minor modes in tonal music. This difference can be formulated as a dependence of the minor mode on the major, for example in that the altered 7th degree in minor can be regarded as a borrowing from the major. Some such dependence is only what one would expect if one presumes an antecedent difference of the major and minor triads based on some relations to overtone-series; if no such difference is presumed, the former difference remains to be explained—or else we have to add still another extra assumption.

From these critiques, Winham constructs his harmonic theory. We can distinguish two basic stages in the development of this phenomenology. Central to an early argument is a conception of *concordance* (and its manifestation in the *integral interval*) that in these writings stands as a sort of phenomenological predecessor to the theoretic notion of consonance: from here he attacks a complex of phenomena such as rootedness, chordal stability, and the construction of proper modes and temperament. This earlier work is fundamentally mathematical: Winham devises a logarithmic index for the phenomena of concordance, tabulates such sums of these values for various combinations of dyads and triads, and constructs appropriate taxonomies.

Although most of this work is not relevant to our further discussion (or will be considered irrelevant inasmuch as it explains facets of the superseding argument), a consideration of one phenomenal domain is important. In his attempt to discover some sort of fundamental rule by which to order concordance, Winham comes to hold a rather interesting and unorthodox conception of the phenomenal logic of octave relations. He first attempts to distinguish octave-equivalence from concordance (a distinction that he grounds in the replication of the even partial series at the octave in the odd partial series). For example [*27c: 2–3]:

> 1. Octave-association is based on something different from, though not necessarily unrelated to, harmonic-series relations. This is clear from its transitivity.
> 2. Nevertheless, the degrees of concordance are degrees of the same phenomenon as that of which the octave, etc., is the highest degree. This must be so since octave-equivalent intervals have the same degree of concordance.
> 3. These facts may seem at first to be in conflict. For if octave-association is based on something different from what concordance is based on, why should they be phenomenally related?
> 4. One answer is as follows: Where octaves are irrelevant (for intervals whose frequency ratio in lowest terms are composed of odd numbers), concordance is simply based on coincidence of series of upper partials. These coincidences also exist for other ratios, of course, and indeed may be more closely related series (to those of the constituent

tones) than in the former cases. But in these cases it is much more obvious that *the fundamental itself of one tone's series is octave-equivalent with an upper partial of the other's series* than that *one of its upper partials is the same as one of the other's series*; and since the latter relation is consequent on the former (but not conversely!) precisely because the *same* relation (as the former) holds *within* the first tones' series, the latter relation becomes merely reinforcement of the former and is not audible separately.

Another plausible answer is that only coincidences of odd-numbered partials have any relevance to concordance, because the octave associations of even numbered partials with lower partials rule them out of independent consideration in relation to other tones; i.e., it is just *because* the octave is so strong a fusion that it is irrelevant for concordance relations between different tones. This is really the same answer actually, but more generally put.

However, these answers really only explain why, for example, the double octave is not perceptible as a weaker concordance than the 12th at the same time that it is an equivalence in some other respect, if it is.

But if the second answer is correct, then the point is that the octave and its powers have the best concordance in terms of odd harmonics alone, for in such an interval, every odd harmonic of either is octave-equivalent with an odd harmonic of the other. Consequently it is quite possible that only odd harmonics have any relevance for a different reason, i.e., not merely because octaves are so closely associated but because even harmonics generally in some sense fail to characterize the tone. A point worth remembering here is that various physical circumstances result in series of only odd harmonics being produced, which therefore a fortiori contain no octaves of the fundamental; yet this synthesis of these into a single tone is just as easy as with octaves, and moreover with greater clarity in that the octave of the fundamental pitch can hardly be mistaken (of course the *even* harmonics alone, incidentally, would produce the wrong period). The series of odd harmonics contains *no* octaves with *any* element; and thus [these harmonics] uniquely fix the *pitch* of every *pitch-class* they represent. Furthermore, the series of the *remaining* (even) harmonics is the same as the series of *odd* harmonics of the period one octave higher.

Therefore I suggest that the role played by odd and even harmonics is actually entirely distinct.

The reason for this may be in the binary system. Here the representation of all powers of $2 \times n$ is of the same shape as that of n itself, which would correspond to octave equivalence. And the special significance of odd numbers is that the mantissa of such a representation is always odd. Furthermore, normal form is simply the form with equal characteristics; the superior tone has the smaller mantissa; and the *root* has the smallest possible mantissa.

Following from this, Winham holds that octave-equivalence or octave-association is in some way logically anterior to concordance. A sense of this construal is given in the following passage [N7: 2]:

> Octave equivalent tones are frequently almost indistinguishable as to pitch if they are in different timbres, even by the most gifted and highly trained musicians. What is still more convincing, however, is that even relations whose significance is a highly indirect consequence of the significance of octave-equivalence are quite obvious. For example, the similarity of sound of the major third and minor sixth, even if none of the four tones involved be identical, which we explain by reference to the operation of transposing one tone by an octave plus the additional transposition of both tones of one pair by a constant. The significance of this relation differentiates the dimension of pitch from, E.G., any Euclidean spatial dimension, by the fact that an arbitrary uniform expansion or contraction of a configuration does not in general preserve all significant relations. (It does not quite follow that absolute interval-size in general is significant, however.)

In other words, Winham here seems to sense that octave-equivalence is to be understood as an abstract quality of pitch space rather than as a quality of pitch events. Within a phenomenal rather than a physical pitch space (i.e., one not marked off by prior specification of steps and intervals defined by frequency) octave-equivalence (as opposed to the simple octave between two pitches) is a logical relation holding between complexes of events. This conception is (incompletely) formalized in a second passage [N36: 17–19] wherein Winham looks at harmonic events not as sums, but as sequences of terms. In the course of this discussion he first specifies that octave-equivalence is a two-place rather than a four-place relation: in other words, it holds between two ordered pairs rather than between all elements of these pairs and hence is a relation of relations. Octave-equivalence is determined by the ordered contiguity of two terms in each of a pair of isomorphic series; octave-similarity by the simple contiguity of two terms in each of the mapped series. Given, for example, two series of partials—C,c,g,c',e' and G,g,d',g",b—the pair C–c would in the narrow and conventional sense be termed "octave-equivalent," yet the ordered pairs c–g and g–d are in a broad sense octave-equivalent. Taken as unordered pairs, they are octave-similar. Hence, Winham does not need to invoke the problematic notions of pitch or pitch-class (as measurable physical events) or any sort of ordered-set counting relation in constructing his conception of the harmonic world: octave-equivalence and octave-similarity phenomenally map relations we would quantitatively speak of as "interval-class" and "interval-type." [Supporting this explication, we read in one manuscript [*67: 7] that the dichords (A–E), (B–E), (A–C) and (B–G) are respectively octave-similar to (C–G), (G–C), (E–G) and (C–E).

The distinction between octave relations (in this broad logical sense) and the qualities of specific intervals (including the octave itself) is crucial to Winham's second theory of harmonic events. Likewise crucial is the realization that interval quality itself need not be explicated in terms of a concordance value but rather can be defined directly against the overtone series. In contrast with his earlier mathematical work on tonal phenomena, the argument that displaces it is strictly axiomatic. (This family of manuscripts in which this axiomatic harmony takes shape includes *1e, *2c, *2d, *2e, *7a, *7b, *14b, *32d, *67, *68, N14, N21, N25, and N36; *14b is given as Pt. 2, Ex. IV.) Thus, in some respects it stands as a direct counterargument to Randall's quasi-axiomatic, set-theoretical argument. In fact, the departure of this formulation from his earlier work is (perhaps) acknowledged in the draft of a note (accompanying what appears to be a very early version of this theory) to Randall [*32d: 1]:

> The following pages contain an outline of what I propose to promulgate this fall as my conception of tonality, and also to publish as part of a long essay or more likely, a book. You will notice immediately how radically it differs both from the approach of your "Draft" and even more from my own approach as of a few years ago. Yet I think that ultimately the differences, though important, do not result in anything that ought to be considered oppositions in the sense of contradiction. The last time I had a sense that there was that kind of disagreement between us was during your weekend blast course, and I now think that in all the points involved then you were right. (I probably remember those points better than you do just because I changed my mind about them.)

The most sophisticated sketch of Winham's phenomenology is assembled in an informal list of definitions. As such, it bears some resemblance to Randall's argument; yet Winham does think of this as the beginning of a full axiomatic system, and other folders hold various additional provisional definitions and theorems of the system. In this particular manuscript, each definition is numbered and occupies a separate half sheet of paper, giving evidence, I think, that this was essentially a work in progress; the whole is dated by Roger Maren as 1968–1969 [*1e: 1–3]:

1. x outlines y: x is a dichordal part of y, and a remainder of y exists and lies between parts of x in pitch.

2. x is an adjacency in y: x is a dichordal part of y such that no part of y lies between parts of x in pitch.

3. x is harmonic with respect to y: x is octave-similar to part of y.

4. x is a step with respect to y: x is dichordal and smaller in pitch span than any dichord which is harmonic with respect to y.

5. x connects y as determined by z: y outlines x and is part of z; dichords in x are steps with respect to z if and only if they are adjacencies in x; every tone x_1 in x forms dichords harmonic with respect to z with each tone in x, except for members of the same pc as tones forming adjacencies in x with x_1; and anything relates to y and z in this way has the same pitches as x.

6. x is a scale (associated with y): x is the sum of connectors of dichords as determined by some sum of pcs, where y has just those pcs; and contains such connectors for every dichord included in that sum of pcs.

7. x is an integral chord (of which y is the fundamental tone): x contains y and some tones of the same pitch as overtones of some tone equal in pitch to y.

8. x is a replete-integral chord: x is an integral chord such that no integral chord equal in pitch-span to x has more pitches.

9. x is of order n: n is the least number of pcs in any replete-integral chord y such that x is harmonic with respect to y.

10. x corresponds in x_1 to y in y_2: x_1 and y_1 have the same number of pitches; x and y are respectively parts of x_1 and y_1 such that for any n, x is the nth-lowest pitch in x_1 if and only if y has the nth-lowest pitch in y_1.

11. x is a consistent representation of y: Any two dichords x_1 and x_2 in x correspond respectively to y_1 and y_2 in y, such that x_1 is smaller, equal, or larger in pitch-span than x_2 if and only if y_1 is respectively smaller, equal, or larger in pitch-span than y_2; x_1 is intervalically equal to y_1 if the latter has only one pc; and these conditions continue to hold if x and y are modified by adding tones one or more octaves above or below corresponding tones in x_1 and y_1 respectively.

12. x is a fundamental chord: x is an integral chord of order (at most) n, where n is the lowest order such that there exist scales associated

with consistent representations of chords of that order. [N.B.—It may be possible to strengthen this, if 3 is the only order having scales of complete chords of that order, which is likely.]

13. x is a complete-fundamental chord: x is a fundamental chord not containing another fundamental chord having more pcs.

14. x is a total chromatic: For each tone y in x, and each complete-fundamental chord z containing y, x contains pitches forming a consistent representation z_1 of z such that y corresponds in z_1 to a tone y_1, equal in pitch to y, in z_1; there are distinct scales in x associated with each such z_1 having a distinct set of pcs; and x contains the minimum positive number of pcs allowing it to satisfy these conditions.

15. x is a tempered-representation of y: x is part of a consistent representation x_1 in a total-chromatic of complete-fundamental chord y_1, and x corresponds in x_1 to y in y_1.

16. x is a primary chord (of which y is a primary tone): x is a tempered-representation of a fundamental chord x_1 having a fundamental tone y_1, and y corresponds in x to y_1 in y_2 [N.B.—The manuscript reads "y_1 in y," but this is surely a mistake.]

17. x is a basic chord (of which y is a direct-root): x has the same pcs as some primary chord (of which y is the same pc as a primary tone).

18. x is diatonic: x is part of a scale associated with a primary chord.

19. x is a segment of y: x contains just those parts of y which lie between two given pitches.

20. x is diatonically equivalent to y: There are diatonic scale segments x_1 and y_1 such that x corresponds in x_1 to y in y_1.

21. x is a tonic of y: x corresponds in a chord x_1 to a direct-root of a diatonically equivalent chord x_2, and y is a scale associated with x_1.

22. x is a root of y: x is a tonic of a scale with respect to its association with a chord containing y.

23. x is definitive with respect to root: A root of x exists and is a root of any chord containing x which has any root.

24. x is consonant: Every dichord in x belongs to a basic chord diatonically equivalent to x.

25. x is a diatonic-octave-equivalent of y: x is diatonically-equivalent to some octave-equivalent of y.

26. The diatonic-deviation of x from x_1 is the same as that from y to y_1: For every dyadic dichord x_2 formed from x_1 and a tone in x, there is a diatonic-octave-equivalent y_2 formed from y_1 and a tone in y, such that x_1 corresponds in x_2 to y_1 in y_2; and vice versa, for every dyadic dichord y_3 formed from y_1 and a tone in y, there is a

diatonic-octave-equivalent x_3 formed from x_1 and a tone in x, such that y_1 corresponds in y_3 to x_1 in x_3.

27. x is in root position (and x_1 is a positional-root of x): The diatonic-deviation of x from a tone x_1 is the same as that of a primary chord y from a primary tone of y.

28. x is a position-determinative tone of y: x corresponds in y to a positional root z_1 of some z in z.

29. x and y are in the same position: The diatonic-deviation of x from a position-determinative tone of x is the same as that of y from a position-determinative tone of y.

30. x is positionally inverse to y: Every dichord x_1 in x corresponds in x to a dichord y_1, which is octave-inverse to x_1, in y.

31. x is in inverse-position: x is positionally inverse to some chord in root-position.

32. x is in intermediary-position: x is neither in root-position not in inverse-position, but is octave similar to chords which are in root-position and to chords which are in inverse-position.

33. x is positionally-determined by y: x is contained in y and contains a position-determinative tone of y.

34. x is potentially more stable than y: x and y are consonant; x is positionally determined by a root position chord and y is not, or neither are, but x is positionally determined by an intermediary position chord and y is not.

35. x is definitive with respect to position: All consonant chords to which x belongs and of which x contains a position-determinative tone are in the same position.

Winham's exposition presumes a set of definitions about pitch relations anterior to the discussion of tonality. The extent of these presumptions is ambiguous: they might include specific pitch (although it might be assumed that this quality is defined in the course of the system—particularly at the point of the seventh definition—by direct comparison with the overtone phenomenon), "pitch-class," and "octave-equivalent" (although, as we shall note, these last two terms are in Winham's thinking more complex than we would expect), yet they would exclude "interval" (whether defined as a quality or as an enumerated span). It is even uncertain whether such a notion as "lower-in-pitch" stands as a unspoken primitive anterior to this harmony (although I believe that it does and that Winham anticipated some continuity between his earlier axiomatized system of pitch and this sketch). Along the same lines, while many of the terms used in the definitions (*tonic*, *root*, and *scale*) correspond to terms of received theory, his exposition demands that we hold any substantive prior conceptions of these terms in abeyance. Winham lays out this sequence very deliberately, a quality that vanishes if we fall back too quickly on received knowledge. The task of reading it is as much one of avoiding contamination as of explication. (In particular, we must avoid conceiving his definitions in terms of equal temperament until the notion of a tempered scale is introduced.)

1. x outlines y: x is a dichordal part of y, and a remainder of y exists and lies between parts of x in pitch.
2. x is an adjacency in y: x is a dichordal part of y such that no part of y lies between parts of x in pitch.
3. x is harmonic with respect to y: x is octave-similar to part of y.

The first two definitions in the sequence—the definitions of "outline" and "adjacency"—require no explication. The third definition presupposes the relationship of octave-similarity.

4. x is a step with respect to y: x is dichordal and smaller in pitch span than any dichord which is harmonic with respect to y.

Thus, the definition of "step" does not need any recourse to a measured class of intervals. If, let us say, y is a dichord spanning a fifth, a dichord spanning a third or even a fourth would constitute a "step." (Of course, when y is a trichord, the definition of "step" is necessarily confined to intervals that do not exceed in size those intervals customarily thought of as steps. In fact, for a trichord composed of two superimposed fourths, a step by this definition would have to be smaller than our "whole-step," a stipulation which makes intuitive sense.)

5. x connects y as determined by z: y outlines x and is part of z; dichords in x are steps with respect to z if and only if they are adjacencies in x; every tone x_1 in x forms dichords harmonic with respect to z with each tone in x, except for members of the same pc as tones forming adjacencies in x with x_1; and anything relates to y and z in this way has the same pitches as x.

Winham's fifth definition seems without complication. The first two clauses (". . . y outlines x and is part of z" and" . . . dichords in x are steps with respect to z if and only if they are adjacencies in x . . . ") are not problematic. With the third clause (". . . every tone x_1 in x forms dichords harmonic with respect to z with each tone in x, except for members of the same pc [pitch-class] as tones forming adjacencies in x with x_1...") we are given to understand that, let us say, a major third within a triad cannot be connected by, let us again say, a superimposed minor third and semitone. Likewise, a fourth within a configuration of two superimposed fourths (such as C–F–B♭) cannot be connected by a series of semitones because of the minor third between nonadjacent tones of the series, which is not harmonic with the reference sonority. In fact, in such a situation no connection of the fourth is possible: this clause very elegantly rules out the connection of two pitches outside of what we might (in received terms) think of as a triadic reference configuration. The final clause (". . . and anything which relates to y and z in this way has the same pitches as x."), however, demands a uniqueness of connection that is not logically entailed by the preceding clauses. For example, if we take a second-inversion triad, it would seem that the fourth could be filled both by sequences composed of any combination of two whole tones and a semitone. Some elucidation of this problem is to be found in a manuscript cited previously (N36) that presents versions of the same material in the form of theorems. This passage opens with three theorems dependent on (at least some earlier version of) Winham's opening sequence of definitions: we do note some variation in terminology, with *pass* replacing *connection*, and *octave-equivalence* substituting for *octave-similarity* (this is the same manuscript that subsequently examines octave-equivalence within a theory of terms), but the general idea stays recognizably the same. (Winham's numerical notation of course refers to the chromatic scale arrayed in a series for 0–11.)

T1. If x is outlined, its parts have at least 3 different pitches.

Proof: By the definition of outlining, x has a part which lies between parts of x. By axiom, any things standing in this relation must all be distinct.

T2. A pass contains parts having at least 3 different pitches.

Proof: By definition, a pass is outlined; combine this with T1.

T3. Suppose z is a consonant triad. Then every associated pass of any given minimal y with respect to z exhibits the same pitches.

Proof: The cases to be considered for y are the dyads of forms 03, 04, and 05. In the case of 03, if z is of the form 037, 013 fails because 17 is not octave-equivalent to any interval of 037, which leaves only 023; if z is 038, 023 fails similarly, leaving only 013. In the case of 04, 0134 fails with respect to 047 because of 17, and with respect to 049 because of 39; this leaves only 024 which works for both triads. In the case of 05, 0145 fails because 14 is both adjacent in y and present in z, whither this is 058 or 059. 0135 and 0235 fail for

z of form 069 because of 39, leaving only 0245; similarly 0135 and
0235 fail for z of form 058 because of 28, leaving only 0135.

This proof is not convincing because it assumes the chromatic
gamut. But the same point can be made another way.

Given a 6/5, 5/4, or 4/3 interval we have to find an intermediary
consonant with the remaining tone of the triad.

Thus consider the dyad $(1, 6/5)$. The only possible intermediary for z: $(1, 6/5, 3/2)$ is 9/8. $(9/9 \times 4/3 = 3/2)$. (The only possible intermediary for z $(1, 6/5, 8/5)$ is $16/15$ $(16/15 \times 3/2 = 8/5)$.) For $(1, 5/4; 3/2)$ we have 9/8. 6/5 is ruled out because it is consonant & so would require another intermediary; but 9/8 cannot serve for that because $5/4 / 9/8$ is not consonant.

For $(1, 4/3, 8/5)$ we have a consonance with 8/5: 16/15, 6/5. This works because $6/5 \times 4/3 = 8/5$. No more can be added here. The other intermediary available is $8/5 / 5/4 = 32/25$ which is non-consonant with 1; & therefore would have to form an adjacency with it. But this is not acceptable because it is larger than 6/5.

If, however, we equate 32/25 with 5/4, then the interval is $5/4 / 16/15 = 5/4 \times 15/16 = 75/64$ which is somewhat smaller than 6/5. [N36; 1–2, 6q]

Of course the proof of this third theorem reinforces the lesson that Winham is not speaking of any sort of tempered reality as yet in his exposition. More important, though, it becomes obvious here that Winham's fifth definition seems to lack one stipulation in its third clause. If we are to change this clause to read "... every tone x_1 in x forms dichords harmonic with respect to z with each tone in x *and z*" the uniqueness of connection in relation to an outside reference posited in Winham's final clause is logically entailed. (A predecessor to this definition appears in a rather different form in what seems an earlier passage [N1: 54]: as one might sense, this particular manuscript focuses directly on Winham's reading of—and reactions to—Randall's *Tonality*.)

1. Let us define a *proper mode-form* as an ordered pair consisting of
   (1) a scale-form x
   (2) a maximal collection of non-adjacencies y, such that every member of x forms one of the (chromatically) *same* intervals *with* some member of y as exist between the members of y themselves.

Next:

6. x is a scale (associated with y): x is the sum of connectors of dichords as determined by some sum of pcs, where y has just those pcs; and contains such connectors for every dichord included in that sum of pcs.

When Winham comes to define "scale" (6), he has already narrowly (and powerfully) specified the context in which a scale can occur. A scale, as an aggregate of connections, can only arise by reference to a triadic sonority, and then is uniquely determined by that sonority. (It would, though, be more accurate in the absence of temperament to speak of a reference sonority as determining not a single scale but rather a *class* of scales. In other words, as Winham has pointed out in this last citation, a connection can manifest itself in an acoustically correct form, an equal-tempered form, or in any number of forms.)

Formally, however, this definition contains a certain lapse. By using the term *pitch-classes* (pcs), Winham brings the notion of octave-equivalence (in the narrow construal) into play without preparation. The grounds for thinking this to be problematic are aesthetic rather than pragmatic: as noted, Winham does presume a basic axiomatic system of pitch anterior to his discussion of harmony, and such a system might well define *pitch-class*. Yet, inasmuch as the beauty of Winham's argument derives from its evasion of an overt description of the structure of pitch space (outside of the broad qualitative construal of octave-similarity), this is troubling.

This lapse, as such, does however open a rather more interesting reading of the passage. Winham's definitions are laid out as a sequence. In that this sequence is provisional, though, we have no reason to presume that this ordering is necessarily fixed (beyond the obvious sequenced introduction of terms). In other words, there is no logical entailment holding between this segment of the sequence (3–6) and the following segment (7–9) that introduces some physical definition of pitch space, and therefore there is no reason for us not to think of these two segments as in some manner logically coterminous.

> 7. x is an integral chord (of which y is the fundamental tone): x contains y and some tones of the same pitch as overtones of some tone equal in pitch to y.
> 8. x is a replete-integral chord: x is an integral chord such that no integral chord equal in pitch-span to x has more pitches.
> 9. x is of order n: n is the least number of pcs in any replete-integral chord y such that x is harmonic with respect to y.

Thus (holding the notions of strict octave-equivalence and pitch-class in abeyance), we find definitions (7) through (9) initiating an autonomous logical sequence. Again, they would seem to require little explication. We have previously enunciated Winham's reasons for turning to a tone–overtone basis for his theory and introduced the notion of the "integral interval" (although his previous conception of the integral interval, with its invocation strictly of the odd partials, is more tightly drawn than this new conception of the integral chord). We might, though, reinforce the notion that Winham looks here for the most minimal assumption on which to base his harmony. This point is rather elegantly made in an earlier working manuscript [N25: 16–17]:

1. The assumption that C and C/G^1 are similar, directly and simply, only when G^1 is an overtone, suggests itself as weaker than the assumption that they always are; and has the advantage of lessening the distinction between C/G and C/G^1.

2. Thus we could combine our ideas and come out with the weakest assumption thus: The primitive similarity is that which holds between chords which differ only as to overtone content, i.e. which have the same predominant pitches. This assumes that predominance is more than merely dynamic; i.e., it presumes that a pitch cannot predominate over another one unless they stand in an integral relation. But it also presumes that even in that case it does not necessarily do so.

It is clear that predominance is different from masking because a masked pitch cannot be heard whereas a subordinate harmonic overtone can be heard by an effort of attention. Thus a subordinate pitch would seem to be one which could be heard but actually is not. This definition, however, would seem to have the consequence that subordinate pitches are irrelevant. But that is not really true. For if we can listen to a prolonged sound and change its characteristics by attention in such a way that the change is of just that kind (and no more) which we know to be correlated with the effort of attention, then we can reasonably conclude that there was an overtone all the time although it was not noticed.

But the mere fact of not being noticed, or of being the root of a thing which is not noticed, is not sufficient to make something an overtone.

Whatever is required beyond this, however, would apparently also apply to the same interval generally.

If we can merely distinguish the relation of being an overtone, we can measure harmonic distance.

Instead of treating 'is an overtone of' as primitive, we may take [the relation] 'of differing only with respect to overtones', i.e., having the same predominant pitches. Now if something has the same predominant pitches, as something which has only one pitch, then it has only one predominant pitch; but it may also have harmonic overtones.

Specifically, we take the relation of differing only with respect to *harmonic* overtones.

In opting for a "weak" recourse to the harmonic overtone series [the "same pitch as" clause in definition (7)], Winham thus intimates that at some stage in the formalization the integral chord could be used as a basis for the definitions of both narrow and broad construals of octave-equivalence and octave-similarity. Definition (9)—like definition (6)—introduces the notion of pitch-class and hence the narrow reading of octave-equivalence, yet here we are in some covert way prepared. It is this coincidence that I think rewards a conception of segments (3) through (6) and segments (7) through (9) as autonomous and even in some way coterminous. In a sense, what Winham gives us is two distinct constructions of pitch space that (in a very loose but complementary way) map onto each other. This picture does not, though, fix octave-equivalence as anything more than an undefined, primitive similarity. Yet, it allows for the two construals of octave-equivalence as phenomenal facts that become important in the next section of the sequence.

10. x corresponds in x_1 to y in y_2: x_1 and y_1 have the same number of pitches; x and y are respectively parts of x_1 and y_1 such that for any n, x is the nth-lowest pitch in x_1 if and only if y has the nth-lowest pitch in y_1.

11. x is a consistent representation of y: Any two dichords x_1 and x_2 in x correspond respectively to y_1 and y_2 in y, such that x_1 is smaller, equal, or larger in pitch-span than x_2 if and only if y_1 is respectively smaller, equal, or larger in pitch-span than y_2; x_1 is intervalically equal to y_1 if the latter has only one pc; and these conditions continue to hold if x and y are modified by adding tones one or more octaves above or below corresponding tones in x_1 and y_1 respectively.

The definition of correspondence (10) is straightforward. The definition of the consistent representation (11) is more demanding. It effectively (particularly in the terminal clause "these conditions continue to hold if x and y are modified by adding tones one or more octaves above or below the corresponding tone in x_1 and y_1 respectively": one must remember that the consistent representation must hold for any x_1 or y_1 in the expanded sonority) fixes the notion of octave-equivalence in a narrow construal that had previously been implied by the notion of "pitch-class" and simultaneously maps some relation akin to what we would term exact transposition. (We should note, though, that in giving a sort of working definition of transposition, Winham still does not draw in some background scale or interval system as an unarticulated primitive.)

12. x is a fundamental chord: x is an integral chord of order (at most) n, where n is the lowest order such that there exist scales associated with consistent representations of chords of that order. [N.B.—It may be possible to strengthen this, if 3 is the only order having scales of complete chords of that order, which is likely.]
13. x is a complete-fundamental chord: x is a fundamental chord not containing another fundamental chord having more pcs.

Winham pulls together these various definitions of scale, integral chord, order, and consistent representation in the definition of the fundamental chord (12). As we might have come to expect, though, this notion itself embodies a good deal of work. For example, we give an earlier definition [*67: 5] of "fundamental chord" that is internally dependent on the definition of "integral interval":

> A fundamental chord of order N is any chord containing a tone X which that every interval (X,Y) in the chord is octave-equivalent to on of the intervals corresponding to the frequency ration $1/1, 3/1, \ldots$ $2N-1/1$. Also the nearest approximation to such a chord in a given gamut may be called a fundamental chord of order N with respect to that gamut, where the qualifying phrase may be omitted if only chords in that gamut are under consideration (except that a chord in a given gamut is only said to have the *lowest* order of any fundamental chord it approximates; e.g. in the 12-gamut the chord (C,E,G) is of course the nearest approximation to infinitely many other octave-equivalents of odd-integral ratios besides 5/1, but is still considered to only be of order 3).

The later definition is rather more subtle, turning on the clause "scales associated with consistent representations of chords..." The notion of an associated scale is consistent with his usage elsewhere, but most important, lest we forget, in line with definition (5) ("x connects y as determined by z") the association of a scale with a particular chord is definitive. His appended note seems (at least heuristically) to be on target, in that (as we have concluded) any dichord that is connected must be no larger than a third, and that hence the integral chord that is represented must contain the fourth partial and must be of order three. A complete-fundamental chord (13) must hence (in received terms) contain all pitch-classes of the triad.

14. x is a total chromatic: For each tone y in x, and each complete-fundamental chord z containing y, x contains pitches forming a consistent representation z_1 of z such that y corresponds in z_1 to a tone y_1, equal in pitch to y, in z_1; there are distinct scales in x as-

sociated with each such z_1 having a distinct set of pcs; and x contains the minimum positive number of pcs allowing it to satisfy these conditions.

This brings Winham to what is perhaps (considering the amount of effort he devotes in earlier manuscripts to questions of temperament, mode, and gamut) the most interesting point in his exposition. Definition (14) of the total chromatic is painstakingly drawn. It follows from definitions (5) and (6) that the fundamental chord needs, by definition, to have an associated *class* of scales. The key phrases are thus, within (14), ". . . x contains pitches forming a consistent representation . . . " and". . . there are distinct scales within x . . .": the last stipulation of the definition ("x contains the minimum positive number of pcs allowing it to satisfy these conditions") being met, the class of scales associated with each fundamental chord becomes a class of one.

15. x is a tempered-representation of y: x is part of a consistent representation x_1 in a total-chromatic of complete-fundamental chord y_1, and x corresponds in x_1 to y in y_1.

16. x is a primary chord (of which y is a primary tone): x is a tempered-representation of a fundamental chord x_1 having a fundamental tone y_1, and y corresponds in x to y_1 in y_2. [N.B.—The manuscript reads "y_1 in y," but this is surely a mistake.]

17. x is a basic chord (of which y is a direct-root): x has the same pcs as some primary chord (of which y is the same pc as a primary tone).

18. x is diatonic: x is part of a scale associated with a primary chord.

19. x is a segment of y: x contains just those parts of y which lie between two given pitches.

20. x is diatonically equivalent to y: There are diatonic scale segments x_1 and y_1 such that x corresponds in x_1 to y in y_1.

The gamut being established, Winham can very easily bring the fundamental chord, by means of the tempered representation (15), into the domain of equal temperament as a primary chord (16). Only now do the higher-level constructions of received theory come into being. Triadic harmony, as such, makes its appearance in the form of the basic chord (17) with a direct root (we remember Winham's notion of "direct" concordance), bringing (18) with its diatonicism (although the "scale" within this system still would not seem to encompass more than six contiguous pitch-classes), and, in the notion of segment (19) a more commonplace understanding of connection, and, in the notion of diatonic equivalence (20) a more accustomed understanding of transposition.

21. x is a tonic of y: x corresponds in a chord x_1 to a direct-root of a diatonically equivalent chord x_2, and y is a scale associated with x_1.

22. x is a root of y: x is a tonic of a scale with respect to its association with a chord containing y.

23. x is definitive with respect to root: A root of x exists and is a root of any chord containing x which has any root.

24. x is consonant: Every dichord in x belongs to a basic chord diatonically equivalent to x.

Thus, the remainder of Winham's argument at first glance presents few problems. In the first portion of (21), the definition of the tonic of a scale, "chords" are of course to be understood as "basic chords," and the "association" of a scale with a chord is loose enough to allow one pitch within a basic chord to function as a tonic for a number of "scales." Following this, the respective definitions of root (22), definitive root (23), and consonance (24), are simply but carefully drawn. The root of a sonority is defined in terms of a chord in which it is contained and that has an associated scale containing a tonic pitch. Together with the notion of definition with respect to root, it seems to rule out any simple neo-acoustic concept of "rootedness." The definition of consonance, so carefully prepared, is thus elegantly economic.

25. x is a diatonic-octave-equivalent of y: x is diatonically-equivalent to some octave-equivalent of y.

26. The diatonic-deviation of x from x_1 is the same as that from y to y_1: For every dyadic dichord x_2 formed from x_1 and a tone in x, there is a diatonic-octave-equivalent y_2 formed from y_1 and a tone in y, such that x_1 corresponds in x_2 to y_1 in y_2; and vice versa, for every dyadic dichord y_3 formed from y_1 and a tone in y, there is a diatonic-octave-equivalent x_3 formed from x_1 and a tone in x, such that y_1 corresponds in y_3 to x_1 in x_3.

27. x is in root position (and x_1 is a positional-root of x): The diatonic-deviation of x from a tone x_1 is the same as that of a primary chord y from a primary tone of y.

28. x is a position-determinative tone of y: x corresponds in y to a positional root z_1 of some z in z.

29. x and y are in the same position: The diatonic-deviation of x from a position-determinative tone of x is the same as that of y from a position-determinative tone of y.

30. x is positionally inverse to y: Every dichord x_1 in x corresponds in x to a dichord y_1, which is octave-inverse to x_1, in y.
31. x is in inverse-position: x is positionally inverse to some chord in root-position.
32. x is in intermediary-position: x is neither in root-position not in inverse-position, but is octave similar to chords which are in root-position and to chords which are in inverse-position.

Then Winham appears to consolidate. The definition of diatonic-octave-equivalence (25) seems simply to expand the definition of diatonic-equivalence (20); and the definition of diatonic-deviation (that we should understand not as some deviation from a diatonic system but rather as a deviation within a diatonic system) would seem simply to strengthen the notion of transposition (26). This itself comes to constitute a rather elegant setup for an economical series of definitions of harmonic disposition: first (27) of root position (remembering, of course, that a primary chord is something different from a basic chord), then (28) of positional determination (in which the root is given an abstract analog) and (29) of positional equivalence, then (30,31) of harmonic inversion and inverse position (a more precise naming of the accustomed "second inversion"), and finally (32) of intermediary position (a more precise naming of "first inversion").

As before, though, the seeming simplicity of this segment conceals a series of difficult and fundamental moves, and I think it admits a richer (if problematic) explication. On second reading, the notion of diatonic-octave-equivalence is puzzling. Again, we do well not to misinterpret Winham's notion of octave-equivalence as a serial rather than a summational relation. Given Winham's definition of diatonic-equivalence (20), which actually precedes his definition of tonic (21) and thus (in our own terms) cannot specify the intervallic equivalence of two scale segments, the relation of diatonic-octave-equivalence simply needs to apply to the relation between two ordinal places in each of two diatonic segments: in other words, the dichord (c–e) could be said to be the diatonic octave-equivalent of the dichord (a–c) in that both occupy comparable ordinal places in comparable diatonic segments. Hence, diatonic-deviation (26) must be measured ordinally rather than acoustically.

Thus, Winham's definition of root position, even in its reference to the primary chord, admits two classes of sonorities, what we would refer to as major and minor chords. We certainly cannot assert that the minor system (as such) could not come into being earlier in Winham's argument: his definition of the tonic of a scale, in its own appropriation of the notion of diatonic-equivalence, quite plausibly applies to minor scales.

This reading is corroborated several times in Winham's writing: he usually speaks of the constituents of the minor system as being "diatonically analogous" to those of the normative major system [*25: 21; N10: 22]. Of course, the belated (or in fact covert) introduction of the minor tonal system may fall short. Yet, there is a sure elegance to this move. Winham is consistent on the derivation of the minor from the major, this assumption being implicit in his choice of the harmonic series as a point of departure for his harmony, and being explicit in his rejection of not simply a naive harmonic dualism but of Randall's grand symmetry of multiple tonal systems. Here, though, he avoids making a point of this difference, to the aesthetic advantage of his argument. Likewise, though, he also avoids arguing a point that (on reflection) is almost too obvious. In short, Winhams's definition of root position avoids completely the calculation of sonority from an arbitrarily specified bass voice. (This point is emphasized in N43: 9.)

Thus, he avoids bringing the quantitative description of interval into the picture. This becomes an important point in the definition of positional inversion (30) and inverse position (31). In developing these definitions [N43: 13–14], Winham first toys with the notion of complementation: "dyadic" here specifies a sonority containing two distinct pitch-classes.

> x is a complementary-inversion of y: Every dyadic dichord x_1 in x corresponds in x to an octave-similar but not octave-equivalent dichord y_1 in y.

> A chord is in inverse-position if it is the complementary-inversion of a root-position chord.

He rather quickly drops the notion of complementation, most likely because of its association with the notion of interval class: to explicitly draw on the notion of interval class would constitute too radical a break from his earlier theories of concordance wherein (as we will remember) two intervals that would perhaps be taken to complement each other (let us say a major third and a minor sixth) would have very different concordance values. He does, however, preserve the abstraction of this argument through the neutral formula of *octave-inverse*. Again, this term stands undefined within Winham's argument, yet, to extend our previous reading of "octave-equivalent," we can hazard that one dichord is octave-inverse to another if it is octave-similar but not octave-equivalent.

33. x is positionally-determined by y: x is contained in y and contains a position-determinative tone of y.

34. x is potentially more stable than y: x and y are consonant; x is positionally determined by a root-position chord and y is not, or neither are, but x is positionally determined by an intermediary position chord and y is not.

35. x is definitive with respect to position: All consonant chords to which x belongs and of which x contains a position-determinative tone are in the same position.

Two of the final three definitions [(33) and (35)] are unproblematic. The definition of potential stability, however, is weak. In fact, we might think of it as the true termination of the series, locating the point where the phenomenology of harmonic events can no longer be isolated from a temporal phenomenology. Winham expends a great deal of energy in the attempt to define stability as a quality (oftentimes as a numerical sum of concordance values), and in its expression as a taxonomy. But here, it would seem, he can go no further inasmuch as the notion of stability is properly the domain of the connectivity between pitch and time worlds (although it implies a logical precedence to pitch, stability being the embodiment of a temporal relation in a pitch quality).

The Phenomenal Structure of Musical Time

Winham does not articulate or construct a phenomenology or musical time commensurable with his phenomenology of harmonic moments. In part, this is because musical time (as he several times points out) is a more elusive or complex phenomenon than pitch and may even be conceived within the musical universe as subordinating pitch. (In other words, pitch may be taken as a function of musical time spans.) Thus, after a point one cannot speak of musical time without invoking pitch in the way in which one could not speak of harmonic events without invoking temporal events.

We can, however, infer the outlines of what such a phenomenology would entail. (This reading, I would emphasize, is far more inferential than my report of his harmonic investigations.) As with pitch, Winham first concerns himself with the question of what would constitute the minimal sufficient primitive or primitives for a system of temporal relations. Unlike with pitch, he finds that an appropriated axiomatic system serves his purposes in part. One interesting folio [*79s] considers an axiomatic system originally developed for biology by J. H. Woodger and later generalized by Carnap as an axiomatic system for spatial and temporal relations, with the attendant problem of defining parts and wholes.[5] A good part of Winham's exposition [pp. 4–9] derives (with minor deviations) directly from Carnap, yet where Carnap assumes three primitives—"part-of," (completely) "earlier," and *"thing"*—Winham drops the last and substitutes the primitive relation "longer," thus adapting the axiom system to the temporal universe of music (dropping any spatial application) and allowing the eventual introduction of the notion of proportion. (The omission of the primitive "thing," of course, might result from the desire to avoid implying the occupation of times by pitch-things at this early stage; although with Carnap time spans themselves are considered "things" in the system, and pitch is later introduced as a function of these things in Winham's system. I think, though, that there is a more interesting reason for this omission, one that I will give in the latter part of this section.)

(As a technical note on my exposition: Carnap gives each formula in the two languages presented in his text, the elementary "A" and the more concise "C." Winham gives each formula in the second of these languages through the definition of "momentary," on which he gives the formulae in the more easily interpreted "A." He also uses a slightly different symbol system, substituting T for Carnap's Tr and MM ("momentary") for *Mom*. My interpretations of formulae are taken, where applicable, from Carnap.)

The system reads as follows. Carnap/Winham first specifies "part-of" as a transitive relation. (For example, if x is a part of y, and y a part of z, x is a part of z.)

A1. Trans (P)

This established, one can define an entity called a "sum" (Carnap) or "sum-individual" (Winham) as a span that itself has parts. (This definition can be read as "x is a sum-individual of a class F provided the elements of F are parts of x, and for each part y of x there is an element z of F such that y and z have at least one part in common.")

D1. $Su(x, F) \equiv \exists (F) \bullet (F \subset P(-,x)) \bullet (y)[Pyx \supset (\exists (z)$
$(Fz \bullet (P \subset P^{-}1)yz]$

[5]Carnap, *Introduction to Symbolic Logic and its Applications*, 213-216.

This definition thereon gives rise to a second axiom designating that every class of temporal events (except the null class) will contain at least one sum-individual.

A2. $F \ni (F) \equiv 1(Su \, (-,F))$

Two theorems apply to the part relation. First, the part relation is reflexive (if x is a part of y, y has a part x), and second, if two individuals are each a part of each other, they are identical.

T1. Reflex (P)

T2. $(P \bullet P^{-1}) \subset I$

Next, there is a relation "earlier" ("T") that is asymmetric. (If x is earlier than y, then y cannot be earlier than x.)

A3. As (T)

If a sum-individual of F is earlier than a sum-individual of G, then F and G are not members of the null class and every element of F is earlier than every element of G. (Winham here gives a variant of Carnap's formula in language "A.")

A4. $(F)(G) \, [(\ni x)(\ni y)(Su(x,F) \bullet Su(y,G) \bullet Txy] \equiv$
$(z)(u)(Fz \bullet Gu \supset Tzu)$

If no part of x is later than y, then any event later than y is later than x; and if no part of x is earlier than y, then any event earlier than y is also earlier than x.

A5. $(P(-,x) \subset \sim T(y, -)) \supset (T(y,-) \subset T(x, , -))$

A6. $(P(-,x) \subset \sim T(-,y)) \supset (T(-,y) \subset T(-,x))$

At this point, Winham's exposition departs from Carnap's model, dropping four theorems (that collectively map out exclusionary relations within the primitive relation "earlier than") and, for some reason, restating A1 as "T3." Winham's fourth theorem (and Carnap's eighth) specifies that the relations "earlier than" and "part of" are mutually exclusive.

T4. $T \subset \sim P$

A temporal event is "momentary" when it cannot be divided into earlier or later parts.

D2. $MM(x) \equiv \sim \ni (T \text{ in } P(-,x))$

Every temporal event has some part that is a moment. (This is the point at which Winham begins stating formulae in Carnap's language "A.")

A7. $(x)(\exists y)(Pyx \bullet MMy)$

Every event has a part (a "slice") that itself has no proper parts and that is a moment: this definition in effect relates moments to non-momentary events. (Carnap at this point introduces his third primitive—"thing"—into the formulae, essentially defining a "thing" as something that can be sliced. This primitive, as noted, is unnecessary to a strictly temporal system.)

D3. $Sli(x,y) \equiv MMx \bullet Pxy \bullet {\sim}(\exists z)(MMz \bullet Pzy \bullet Pxz \bullet x{\neq}y)$

After again dispensing with two of Carnap's theorems (which demonstrate the exclusivity of slices) Winham returns to the definitions of "initial slice" and "end slice."

D4. $ISli(x,y) \equiv Sli(x,y) \bullet (z)[Sli(z,y) \bullet (z{\neq}x) \supset Txz]$

D5. $ESli(x,y) \equiv Sli(x,y) \bullet (z)[Sli(z,y) \bullet (z{\neq}x) \supset Tzx]$

At this point, Winham's system diverges from Carnap's exposition, introducing his own third primitive, "longer." (I have been unable to locate this extension in any other outside text, although I would not rule out the possibility. The interpretations of the remaining formulae are my own.) Two events stand in the relation "equal length" when neither is longer or shorter.

D6. $EL \equiv (L \vee L^{-1})$

The relation "longer" is transitive and asymmetric.

A8. $Trans \bullet As(L)$

"Equal length" is transitive.

A9. $Trans (EL)$

It is thus reflexive and symmetrical.

T5. $Reflex \bullet Sym (EL)$

An event is "temporally continuous" if (through an infinite regression) it contains two ordered slices and some other thing that stands between them, and thus also contains some slice that also stands between them.

D7. $TCx \equiv (y)(z)[Sli(y,x) \bullet Sli(z,x) \bullet Tyz \bullet (\exists w)(Tyw \bullet Twz) \supset$
$(\exists u)(Sli(u,x) \bullet Tyu \bullet Tuz)]$

Two events are "temporally contiguous" if neither is (wholly) earlier than the other and if there is a sum-individual that contains both events and is temporally continuous.

D8. $CTxy \equiv (T \lor T^{-1})xy \bullet (Su(-,\{x,y\}) \subset TC)$

An event is defined as a "contiguity-class" if for any event it contains there is some other event to which the first is temporally contiguous, and that contains two other nonequivalent events that are neither (wholly) earlier or later than each other, or it is a single class of events, which are temporally continuous.

D9. $Ctg(F) \equiv [(x)(Fx \supset (\exists y)(Fy \bullet CTxy)) \bullet (z)(u)(Fz \bullet$
$Fu.(z \neq u) \supset (T \lor T^{-1})zu] \lor [1(F) \bullet F \subset TC]$

Winham's final definition moves the calculus onto more familiar phenomenal ground. He reads the formula as "x and y are in (length) proportion M/N." (Carnap uses the formula "Str$_1$Induct" to indicate mathematical induction: Winham notes that the attempt to interpret this definition would only confuse matters, yet should we venture for a more detailed interpretation of the formula, we might say that two events x and y are in length proportion M/N if given two contiguity-classes F and G that are equal in length to x and y respectively, and that respectively contain some parts z and u that are equal in length, and from which we can strongly induce that two undefined quantitative entities M_1 and N_1 apply respectively to F and G, then the product of M and N_1 and the product of M_1 and N must agree. The key move in this formula is the specification of some z and some u that are parts of the contiguity classes F and G and that are equal in length: this allows the comparison denoted by the strong induction.)

D10. $LProp (M,N,x,y) \equiv (F)(G)(M_1)(N_1) [[Ctg(F) \bullet Ctg(G) \bullet F$
$\subset EL(x,-) \bullet$

$G \subset EL(y,-) \bullet (\exists z)(\exists u)(Su(z,F) \bullet Su(u,G) \bullet EL(z,u) \bullet$
$Str_1 Induct (M_1) \bullet$

$Str_1 Induct (N_1) \bullet M_1(F) \bullet N_1(G)] \supset [Prod(M,N_1) =$
$Prod(N, M_1)]$

Winham introduces his last axiom in order to convert "length-proportional" into a function (there being some pairs of individuals for which there may be no rational proportion). It should be read as "x is in the same proportion to y as z is to w." It can be interpreted as "given individuals x and y, and classes M and N and M_1 and N_1, if M and N are length-proportional to x and y respectively, and M_1 and N_1 are also length proportional to x and y, then they are length-proportional to each other.

A10. $(x)(y)(M)(N)(M_1)(N_1)$ [LProp(M,N, x, y) • LProp $(M_1, N_1,$ x, y) $\supset$ $(M = M_1 • N = N_1)$]

The applicability of this axiomatic series to a phenomenology of musical time is obvious. By first defining time spans as sum-individuals possessing parts (or more accurately, making this definition available to time spans by introducing the ordering primitive "earlier"); by introducing the defining notions of initial and end slices, this calculus makes possible (if one were to extend it) the concept of a rational (although not a real) metric, one in which the notion of regular division is introduced by the comparison of time spans. (Thus, it might be that metric space can be argued axiomatically by the subdivision of one span by another into parts: I think it is important to point out that due to performance inflections, accelerandos, and the like, to say nothing of sudden tempo changes, argue against a rigid notion of metric time.) In this respect, Winham's additional definitions of the relations "temporally continuous," "temporally contiguous," and "(length-) proportional" strengthen this hypothetical extension. (Any student of 14th- and 15th-century European music is well aware of the possibilities of proportion.)

But I think that Winham takes the basic relations defined in this series in a different and richer direction (if through an informal and nonaxiomatic argument). In fact, I believe that his strategy in elaborating a phenomenology of musical time is somewhat akin to that he takes in developing his phenomenology of the harmonic moment. In the latter, his basic argument from the primitive "lower than" could easily have lead to a sort of Randall-system, yet he preferred to introduce instead the more difficult but phenomenally rich primitive of the overtone series. Here, he cannot determine a corresponding primitive from which to construct even a quasi-formal argument, yet he does submerge his axiomatized temporality in a correspondingly rich account of musical experience (although this is not immediately apparent).

In a single manuscript (it is rare that an idea occurs only once in Winham's writings, so we are here speaking of a line of reasoning that is not brought to the surface), dissatisfied with his definition of the musical work as an "extensional" or "intentional" predicate or the like, he asserts a new definition. This definition relies on the account of temporal asymmetry we have encountered earlier (i.e., given a piece of music with the ordering of events AABA, for example, we by virtue of memory hear pieces A, AA, AAB, and AABA.) Under this new definition, the work ("W") is no longer a single entity but an ordered series of time spans initiated at the beginning of the piece and terminating at every moment within the piece [N19: 221–222]:

> We might replace the one configuration W, satisfying W, with a sequence of partial configurations with W as the last term. Then by defining 'the work' not as W but as a class of such ordered sets of configurations having a member of W as the last term, we introduce the time-ordering on the structural level.
>
> This procedure seems somewhat overcomplicated, in as much as (1) the time-relations now appear in two different ways, (2) if what is desired is that the time-order be regarded as structural, it would suffice to give the structure as the ordered set of the sets of events at each time point, this ordering being the time-order. But this latter procedure presupposes that there are *minimal* events.
>
> The answer to objection (1) may be that this is just what we want. For while time-relations and other qualities are comparable in some ways, they are essentially different in one way, and just this way is what is expressed by our definition.
>
> Nevertheless it may be that another method will do so more clearly. One approach would be to specifically include "memory-images" as values of the variables, and to demand that every event be *simultaneous* with a "memory-image" of every previous event. But this seems still more complicated.
>
> Our first proposal has the advantage of clearly *showing* the asymmetry of the temporal situation. For each ordered set belonging to a work, its inverse set is of course *not* a member of the retrograde-work, but on the contrary, is a member of some work which could not be experienced except by a being whose time was inverse to ours. The next question is whether it adequately expresses the sense in which simultaneity is an indestructibly associative factor, as opposed to other qualitative identities. The point here would be that *if and only if two events are simultaneous*, they belong to all the same members of our ordered set.

This representation presupposes (as does Carnap's series of propositions) a nonmetric definition of time. The first objection in the second paragraph ("the time relations now appear in two different ways") makes reference to Winham's two primitives, "earlier" and "longer": to propose an ordered series is to suppose that terminal points of each span obey this relation, yet the spans themselves are simultaneously related by length; hence his statement that this may be just what we desire. His second objection, that the work might just as well be described as an ordered set of the sets of events, and hence leads to the notion of a minimal event, is a caution against the introduction of a temporal metric at this stage. (I would not here draw from the phrase "introduce time-ordering on the structural level" any intimation of the structural levels of pitch function: Winham merely wishes to eliminate the possibility of a discrete and finite ordering according to event size.)

It is at this juncture, though, that Winham's account becomes most interesting.

> A point that might be raised is whether it is necessary that the set be *ordered*, since its order can in any case be shown by the temporal extent of the members, or what is the same, by their inclusion relations.
>
> This criticism seems valid. We may replace the ordered set by simply the set.
>
> We still have to meet the difficulty of avoiding the assumption that events have a minimal size and more particularly, of avoiding the assumption that one minimal event cannot extend beyond another in both temporal directions. This latter assumption, however, is probably unavoidable in any case. In particular, there seems to be no disadvantage in assuming that if the beginning of an event x precedes the beginning of y, but the end of x does not precede the beginning of y, then x has a part which ends either before or at the same time as the beginning of y. In short, the occurrence of y makes x divisible even if it would not be otherwise. In this case the difficulty disappears, as if two events cannot be ordered, at least one of them must be non-minimal. The first difficulty still has to be met, however. But this is easy: the set of events which count as before or simultaneous with a given one in our sense are all those which end before or at the same time as it ends.
>
> This might be called the 'univalent theory of time', in that while it does not decide whether there are instants, it insists that an event must have a part exactly correspondent with any event beyond which it extends in both temporal directions. In a sense it is a logical theory: it postulates the *correspondent* part as a logical necessity.

By considering the collection of all possible "memory-image" spans as an unordered collection, we are immediately given a phenomenal ground for the notion of parts (inasmuch as given any two such spans that are nonidentical, one must determine parts of the other), and thus ground for the relations "earlier than" and "longer than": the rest of the propositional sequence follows from this. The notion of parts, if we are to treat them in turn as sum-individuals, also gives ground for considering spans that are not members of the set of "memory-image" spans but that can function within the piece themselves as collections of "memory-image" spans (if of a subordinate order).

Of course the notion of these "memory-image" spans, all of which are initiated at the opening of the piece, as an unordered collection is counterintuitive. Winham allows it because he is not describing a psychological process of memory but defining a thing called a "work." Taken as such, though, it does connect to a certain class of almost fugitive musical intuitions. To use an example (of which Winham would probably disapprove), it gives us ground for understanding why a "surprise" in a piece remains a surprise even on repeated hearing: simply put, our consciousness of the work always includes a collection of spans at which this "surprise" is not a part. In the course of hearing the work, even after repeated hearings, we still cannot step outside of the members of the set of partial pieces that are part of the definition of the work (although it conversely cannot be "unknown" that the "surprise" lies definitely in some future piece span). Likewise, though, it gives us some grasp of the idea of getting to know the piece through repeated hearings: "knowing" a piece is equivalent to holding the entire unordered collection of "memory-image" spans.

But it is impossible to carry this line of reasoning further without speaking of pitch. Reinterpreting Carnap's axiomatic argument, we might note that the concept of a slice gives ground for the definition of the harmonic slice (that Winham has so ably unpacked) of the work (in the above sense of the term) in which pitch constitutes a function of time spans. (This notion would of course require a great deal of work to bring it to the stage of being an acceptable argument.)

The formula "memory-image span" and the particular piece world it opens up are suggestive particularly of Schenker's "hearing at a distance." The picture of a simultaneously given collection of these spans is likewise suggestive. Given the notion of pitch as a function of time span, we would be remiss in not reviewing (if only superficially) Winham's conception of functional pitch spans. His take on the Schenkerian analysis derives, as we expect, from that of Milton Babbitt [*13a: 1].

> Thus while many saw in Schenker's 'reduction' of tonal music through various levels to an elementary background only an attempt to legislate all music into essential identity, Babbitt realized that

Schenker's critical importance lay precisely in this supposedly objectionable aspect of his theories, because the Schenkerian 'techniques of composition' could be regarded instead as the operations of an analytical system, and thus Schenker's theory of how music should be composed could be translated into an empirical theory of how it was in fact composed by a certain group of composers, not in the sense that the techniques were compositional procedures, but that they corresponded to operations or inference-rules of a recursive definition of this type of music.

For Babbitt (or Babbitt as reported by Winham) Schenker's analysis of music is necessarily reconceived as a descriptive and analytic system rather than a prescriptive system. (One might argue with Babbitt—or Babbitt reported by Winham—on this point, particularly given our notion of Schenker's work as an analytic system. Yet, it may be that our own reading of Schenker is an unacknowledged artifact of this move.) For Winham, the critical strategy turns on the abstraction of compositional techniques as a discrete series of operations recursively applied. To what they are to be applied is somewhat at issue. For now, it will suffice to posit that they applied to pitches: Winham usually takes the pragmatic course and assumes the individual tone as the element in a system of tonal operations [i.e., *4: 18–31]. (This is something we will pick up again in the next section.)

The operations, as given by Winham, derive from the techniques of strict counterpoint. Winham gives an informal list of operations (one among several in his writings) in the text of a lecture on the opening of Beethoven's Sonata Op. 27, No. 2 [N23:21–22]:

> One may divide the operations into categories according to the amount of change they effect, thus
>
> > I. Purely articulative operations. These merely substitute a fresh attack (repetition), or a rest, for some part of a tone other than its beginning; or extend the tone.
> > II. Delays and anticipations (of single tones). These affect the exact time at which a pitch occurs, but still do not introduce completely new pitches. (The difference from type I is that type-I operations do not affect the initial attack-time of a pitch).
> > III. Octave doublings and transfers (of single tones). These affect the pitches but not the pitch classes.
> > IV. Chromatic inflection. Here a new tone is substitute for some part of a tone, but the two pitches are the same number of steps from some third tone, by virtue of different diatonic Scales. Thus here the pitch is changed, but not the diatonic interval to the third tone.

When the two Scales involved are coordinate scales, the chromatic inflection is also called a mixture (of major and minor).

V. Path-connections. This is the only type introducing essentially new material, in the sense of new diatonic intervals. There are two main sub-types:

(a) Passing-tone connection. Here the operand configuration is a direct succession of two tones of different pitches. The operation shortens the first tone and replaces its latter part with a succession of 'passing tones' of increasing or decreasing pitch so as to connect the (remnant of) the first tone with the second tone by a series of steps along some diatonic scale. Thus the result is a statement of a path in order of pitch. The path may or may not be determined by a chord actually occurring at the same time, but that would be the most normal case.

(Note: chromatic inflection may also result in a similar configuration if the third tone immediately follows and is a step in the same direction as the preceding inflection; hence the term chromatic passing-tone is applied to such an inflection. However in this case the interval between the thus connected tones is itself a diatonic step; the passing-tone proper uses such steps to connect the larger interval).

(b) Neighboring motion. Here the non-final part of a tone to, or the latter part of an immediately preceding tone, or even an immediately preceding silence, is replaced by a tone which is a diatonic step away from it. Thus (a remnant of) it always follows the new tone (the 'neighbor'). It may but need not also precede the neighbor (i.e. the neighbor may replace a part out of the middle of it); if it does, the result is called a complete neighboring motion.

This list is possibly not exhaustive (it depends on the boundaries of what we choose to call 'tonal' music; the intention is to list the standard types of operation used in classical music fairly narrowly so termed). Also some particular sub-types and compounds occur much more frequently than others, or are for some other reason worthy of having special names. These include:

(1) Arpeggiation. This belongs to type II, and consists of converting a chord, i.e. simultaneous sounding of two or more pitches, into an immediately successive sounding of the same pitches. The basic importance of this lies in the fact that it creates the successions to which V(a) can then be applied to obtain new pitches (Ex. [2]).

(2) Suspension. This is similar to arpeggiation in that one element of a chord is delayed; however, in this case a preceding tone is also

held longer, filling the gap which would otherwise occur because of the delay. The latter (new) part of this tone has a different pitch than was originally at that time-point, so that this operation may be considered to belong to type V; what this means in practice is that the interval from the held to the delayed tone is usually a diatonic step, so that the only difference from the incomplete neighboring motion is that the neighbor is here also the latter part of a tone arising in some other way. (Ex. [1] (3)). The new part of the held tone is called the 'suspension', and the following delayed tone its 'resolution'.

Several points in this taxonomy bear remarking. First, Winham orders his operations in terms of the amount of change they effect. The passing and neighbor motions, the most primitive of the contrapuntal operations, are the most powerful of the operations.

Second, in citing "articulative operations" and "delays and anticipations" as the least powerful of his operations he makes obvious the rhythmic content of the operations as a whole: delays and anticipations and articulative operations are presumed to have their effect on proper elements that already have some sort of temporal expression. (In fact, it may be at the level of these minor operations that the rhythmic metric comes into being.) In a second such taxonomy [*13c; Pt. 2, V], he reconfigures these two operations as four: subdivision (the division of the duration of the tone into a prime number of equal segments), suppression (the omission of a tone under carefully delineated circumstances), merger (the converse of subdivision), and tie and anticipation (the extension of a tone through another tone, either preceding or following, that has been subdivided and suppressed). Rhythm, in Winham's system of tonal operations, defines the operation fully as much as does pitch, and even at this elementary stage it is unsure whether rhythm is the temporal expression of pitch structures or the pitch expression of temporal structures. (Thus, the description of the rhythm of passages that evidence tonal operations is as important as the description of pitch, and "background" rhythmic structures are as important as pitch structures. Winham usually assumes a rhythmic background articulated in equal-values and then subject to complex displacements.)

Third, some operations are compounds of other operations. Thus, in his first taxonomy, arpeggiation is taken as a delay: in the second taxonomy it is taken as a function of the suppression of one or more tones of the harmonic entity. The first reads suspension as a compound of a delay and a path connection; the second gives it as a compound of a suppression and a tie or extension.

Winham, however, would make here a fourth point. He would point out that none of these descriptions are adequate for the purposes of defining operations. The operations are functions: each alteration of pitch posits a distinction between superior and inferior tones, a distinction Winham at times terms aptly a "containment relation" [*3a, *16a, *19, *4]. This is obvious in the case of the passing motion, the neighbor, the suspension, and more complex in the case of the anticipation: to determine a superiority relation for the latter, we have to bisect the tone itself and consider the initial part to be inferior to the terminal part.

(In his description of operations, Winham also recognizes a number of harmonic and prolongational techniques not recognized in strict counterpoint, speaking of tonal "tendencies." Accepting some heuristic formulation of tendency, this same relation might even apply to the arpeggiation: for example, given a tendency of bass arpeggiation to move downward, we might consider such an operation to be a containment relation—as it clearly is in the case of the fifth. Clearly the dominant cadence is a containment relation. I avoid dealing here with these sort of operations in part because the contrapuntal operations are relatively more definite in Winham's theory and also in part to limit the scope of the discussion.)

This simple taxonomy of operations is, however, the subject of two intriguing critiques. The first [N19: 195–200; Pt.2, VI] questions the working of these operations on logical grounds. Winham begins this critique with the idea that an operation can be defined by a set of minimal necessary conditions, for example, that a passing motion can be defined by specifying a set of elements in a particular temporal order within which the step relation obtains between contiguous elements and these step relations are all in the same direction. He next argues that it is probably not possible to analyze a piece in this way, even if we were to add any number of conditions to our definition. Analysis actually entails a different sense of the operation, one that defines the minimal necessary conditions that at a certain level in a correct analysis (rather than in general): in other words, the definition of an operation is contextual in the sense that it changes according to where it is situated in the analysis. But it might also be necessary to specify in which analysis such a definition holds inasmuch as there are at least a certain class of analyses of the same text that are all correct or adequate. Moreover (and this is the heart of the matter), it would be necessary to determine some criteria for judging the particular analysis as correct or adequate. Winham's own statement of his conclusions is perhaps more vigorous than my own. (The subscripts "1" and "2" refer to two different senses or levels of the operations. "He" refers to Schenker.)

> By this of course I do not mean that he confused, e.g., 'passes$_1$' with 'passes$_2$'—this would have been too crude a mistake. But he did think that by adding further conditions and riders to "Subscript-'1'" terms, as we did in defining P$_1$, he could arrive at a general definition of 'passing$_2$'. And this still seems to be the general view of those who do Schenkerisations—for while they are always producing complicated and obscure reasons why 'passes' does or does not hold in some given case, they hardly ever consider the general question of what makes one Schenkerisation preferable to another, and even when they do there is certainly no hint of any belief that the meaning of 'passes' might depend on this question. But if, as seems obvious, the latter question in turn depends on that of what, in general, makes one analysis of any piece better than another, then there is clearly no reason to believe that 'more-adequate-Schenkerisation-than' is definable in terms of "Subscript-'1'" terms; and hence there is no reason to believe that "Subscript-'2'" terms are definable in terms of "Subscript-'1'" terms; and in particular, 'passes$_2$' is almost certainly not definable in terms of "Subscript-'1'" terms, no matter how complicated the conditions are made. *Thus the reason that no one has been able to clearly specify the conditions under which a tone is or is not a passing tone is not just that it is a very difficult problem, but that in the sense of 'conditions' and 'passing' in use, the problem is in principle insoluble.* If Schenker-style analysis is to be clarified, we must choose between (A) using only the "Subscript-'1'" language, and accepting the consequence that all such questions as whether a given tone is or is not a passing tone (except in the trivial sense of "passes$_1$') must simply be shelved as irrelevant, and (B) attempting to explicate the general notion of better-analysis-than. Any other course is doomed to eternal confusion.

If, though, we are unable to arrive at a definition of, let us say, "passing tone," which remains stable between the contrapuntal exercise and the middle-ground or background analysis (even if we are to amend the first definition to let it function at the different level), how do we recognize operations when we hear them? Holding the notion of better analyses in suspension, we get some answer to our first question in Winham's second critique. This argument, given (uncharacteristically again) in only one text [N2: 68–71; Pt. 2, VII], draws obliquely on the "memory-image" time-span construal of the musical work. The tonal operation, as stated before, can be conceived as a function. Winham turns to the phenomenal content of such a function. Given, let us say, a neighbor operation, we do not perceive it as a function until the inferior tone appears, and identify it until the appearance of the second superior tone appears. Thus, the primarily affected time span of the operation includes only its final two elements, and the time span of the entire operation is to varying degrees indeterminate (in that the span of the first superior tone can be in practice distributed over several tones), and the temporal sense of the operation is asymmetric. The substance of Winham's own words is worth repeating [N2: 69]:

> The *primarily affected time-span* of a linearly subordinate element is the time from its beginning until the beginning of the next element in the series generated by the operation, or the main element in the case of a minimal motion.
>
> This time-span thus varies according to what we consider the next element to be; on the other hand, what we consider the original main tone (or previous element in the series of a non-minimal motion) to be has no effect on the time-span, because this cannot begin before the element concerned is begun. In practice we must usually consider several different time-spans for the same element, because typically tonal music distributes the various plausible qualities of a main tone for a given element over several different subsequent tones.
>
> In this sense the time-span of a complete progression has an *essential* main tone (the one that comes at the end and thus defines the time-span of the subordinate tone) and an *inessential* main tone (the one which comes at the beginning and does not affect the subordinate span).
>
> In the case of the neighbor, the inessential main tone is also inessential in the sense that it need not occur at all; this is not true for the passing progression, because the initial main tone is essential to define the interval through which the tones pass (it is perhaps conceivable, nevertheless, that this tone might be omitted by an inferior operation; but I know of no clear case where this analysis seems plausible). In other words, a neighbor may be applied by replacement of the initial segment of the main element. Theoretically it might also replace the terminal segment; but in this case it would have an indefinitely extending time-span. Hence this is most plausible at the end of a piece.
>
> A justification for this asymmetrical view of the definition of time-spans might be found in the mere fact of the attack of a tone coming at its beginning. I.e., if we consider time-spans as defined only by attacks, then the time-span of a progression runs from the attack of the first main element to the attack of the final one, and the subordinate

element in a minimal progression is then more closely associated with the final main element in that its time-span occupies the final segment of the progression.

This argument has problems in particular cases, however (e.g. a succession of staccatos).

Instead, we should appeal to the concept of effective context. The final main tone (or 'resolving tone') includes the subordinate tone in its effective context, while the original main tone does not. Or better: the (subordinate tone + final main tone) has the same effective context as the main tone by itself; by one of our basic assumptions, this is a similarity—indeed the analogy with the relation of derivative to root is obvious (the similarity of part to whole). On the contrary, however, the (original main tone + subordinate tone) has the same effective context not as the main tone but as the subordinate one. For this reason it may be argued that in every succession of two events there is a ground for regarding the second as the 'main ' one, i.e. that it has a similarity to the sum.

Pragmatically, this means that we still perceive the function if the first tone is omitted in its entirety, giving, let us say, an unprepared neighbor or suspension (although then the two may be locally indistinguishable): the passing tone does of course still require two superior tones for us to perceive it as such. It also gives us some idea of how a pitch can be left "hanging" (the effective context embracing two pitches being interrupted by a superior context). Most interestingly, though, it leads at the close of Winham's argument to a definition of a familiar entity:

> It could be argued that if we are going to consider the piece as a set of effective contexts, then each such context ought to be viewed as having its last events *nearest* in time. This relation would be similar to emphasis. This is very likely correct; but there still may be a simpler method which is not incorrect.
>
> In answer to this argument, in any case, it could be argued that there is a fundamental distinction between presence and absence only; that temporal remoteness, beyond this, is not fundamental. And since an effective context, i.e., a time, is identified by its last or present events, there is not need to make any further distinction.

The musical piece—for example, the musical "work"—is here defined in terms of the "effective time spans" of the containment relations of pitches. Obviously this conflicts with the earlier definition of the musical work as the class of memory spans (each defined as that time holding between the initial slice of the piece and another slice, each exclusive). I think, however, that Winham's phenomenology of musical time (or one implicit in his reasoning) is to be discovered in the reconciliation of these two definitions.

In the definition of the musical work, the set of time spans is unordered. In other words, at some place we hold pieces that we know not as a series of events but rather as a dense collection of temporal intuitions, or (in Winham's words) "memory spans." To expand on this, one might go so far as to say that the vividness of this collection of memory spans is heightened by our familiarity with the work. But in the course of listening to the work, the containment operations create effective time spans or (to rename them) "proper memory spans," which by a sort of pseudocomparison with the real memory spans themselves create virtual partial works. This does not, of course, rule out their coinciding with real memory spans (if they are in some way initiated at the beginning of the piece). These proper memory spans, though, are in fact not defined as are true time spans: they may have but do not require an initial slice. (This, I believe, explains the puzzling omissions in Winham's redaction of Carnap's axiom system. Winham, as we may remember, leaves out Carnap's primitive "thing." The most plausible reason for this is that he wishes to avoid Carnap's axioms [8] and [9], which state that every "thing" has at least one initial slice and one end slice. The proper time span, of course, does not need an initial slice.)

Taking things further, this phenomenology intimates a contingent solution to Winham's problem of the "more-than-adequate" analysis. If the collection of proper memory spans represents in some way the set of real memory spans, if the set of proper memory spans best represents the set of real spans if it contains spans of a large range of sizes, and if these proper memory spans need not have an initial slice, they must have some means of representing virtual size through their real inferior and superior elements. Thus, the efficacy of proper memory spans is dependent on having a range of definition for the tonal operations.

Hierarchies, Ambiguity, and the Relation of Theory to Analysis

The phenomenal construction of musical time put forward in the previous section is a conjectural extrapolation from a limited body of texts of which only a small portion is given in axiomatic form. I believe, however, that it would be expressible within an axiomatic system, and, more important, that the assumptions of such a phenomenology are implicit in a further domain of Winham's writings.

Certainly, though, it says little about the appearance of a real (as opposed to rational) metric in most music. The symmetry of such real metrics argues against their being introduced too early into the asymmetrical phenomenology. (Interestingly, the dependence of the former on the latter in Winham's thinking is indicated in one text where he proposes that tonal rhythm—the unfolding of pitch events in a rational metric—is undeniably asymmetrical. In other words, the inversion of a durational figure such as a dotted eighth note followed by a sixteenth note completely changes its meaning: a sixteenth note followed by a dotted eighth strongly marks the operation of anticipation, a low-priority and hence more "surface" operation.) Perhaps in a way similar to that in which discrete pitch comes into being within Winham's system through the operation of tempering the "rational" space defined by the overtone series (which, like the temporal space of Winham's memory spans, is bound at one extreme yet infinite), the metric space of tonal music might arise out of a 'tempering' or the rational metric: inasmuch as the tactus in tonal music is not absolute (i.e., such operations of performance as rubato, accelerandos, and any number of changes of tempo do not affect our perception of a pulse), it may be that the ear will accept the compromise of a real metric in order to make various rational time spans comprehensible.

The problem with these speculations, though, is that Winham views a real metric as present in even the simplest example of the connection between pitch and temporal domains. In his analysis of musical texts (rather than his phenomenological analysis: we will distinguish these two investigations as the "analysis of texts" and the "analysis of phenomena") even the most primitive of operations such as the unfolding of a passing tone over the bass arpeggiation of the *Ursatz* are defined against a real metric, and such purely rhythmic operations as anticipation and delay (suspension) make their appearance quite early in the explication of any particular foreground.[6]

The same analytic procedure, however, provides some clues as to the relation of rational and real metrics in Winham's theory of tonal music. Absent a complete and explicit analysis of phenomena, one in which a fully axiomatic phenomenology of harmonic events and a cor-

---

[6]A detailed development of the notion of the metric middle ground is given in Arthur Komar's *Theory of Suspensions: A Study of Metrical and Pitch Relations in Tonal Music* (Princeton: Princeton University Press, 1971). Komar, as noted in the introduction, was a student of Godfrey Winham, and this book (which is derived from his dissertation) is deeply indebted to Winham's analytic procedure (although many of the ideas contained therein and their development are certainly Komar's).

responding phenomenology of musical time give rise to a phenomenology of their connectivity, Winham relies in his textual analysis on a simpler picture of musical relations. He attempts in one text [*26d; Pt. 2, VIII] to incorporate these observations into a sort of analytic protocol. This theory of textual analysis displaces a simpler theory in which individual tones were to be assigned a sort of "index of level": in other words, tones in the analysis that were remnants of the original sonority (however much they were shifted or displaced in the course of succeeding levels) would be assigned a level designation, for example, "E^0" or "D^1." The way in which this new protocol differs from its predecessor is very important. The sequence begins with the definition of the elements of the system and their qualities:

> 01. Each tone has various functions, which are divided (1) into Necessary and Unnecessary (always capitalized to avoid confusion with the simple root-meanings, though these are related), and (2) into a hierarchy of Higher and Lower functions, which, however, is not simply a series but a more complicated structure, as will be seen. This hierarchy applies only to the Necessary functions in the first instance; a similar hierarchy could be described for the others, but this will not be done here and would be of less significance.

Leaving aside the notion of hierarchies, the important point made here is that the elements of the analysis of texts are specific tones (events defined as to pitch and length) rather than sounds and time spans (as in the analysis of phenomena). As given in another text [*30ba: 6; Pt 2, IX]:

> In this much, we are in essential agreement with J.R., i.e., we agree that the statements of reductive analysis are statements about the foreground, not about how it was or could have been constructed. It follows, as he says, that the 'notes' of higher levels are actually parameters of the foreground notes, however indirectly (it *does not* follow that they have no 'durations'; they can just as well have these as 'pitches' obviously).

Returning to the protocol [*26d], the functional qualities of these elements are defined as the product of the various tonal operations that govern certain time spans (including, for Winham harmonic and rhythmic containments in addition to the classical contrapuntal operations), these time spans here being termed *locales*:

> 02. Each function determines a group of tones, in relation to which the function exists. Such a group will be termed a locale. Each locale is a locale-of-function of each of its constituent tones.

The nature of a locale determines relations of Superiority or Inferiority among its constituent tones, thus: A tone x is inferior to another y if there exists a locale in which the relation of x to y is a Necessary function of y but not of x .

It is evident that of a given pair of tones, neither need be superior, as there may be no locale which is a locale of function of both. Moreover there may exist two different locales including both x and y, such that x is both superior and inferior to y. However, in all such cases one of these locales is a sub-group of the other, and the subgroup is an incomplete locale in the sense defined below. Thus with this rare but important exception, superiority of x to y excludes the reverse relation.

03. All incomplete locales are such that they would remain (correct) locales if other tones were added; but this cannot be used as a definition because there exist cases of extendible complete locales. The following definition is correct: a locale is incomplete if one of its temporally outer tones is inferior to another of its tones. Thus a complete locale is one in which the temporally outer tones have no superiors in the locale. The relations of inferiority referred to must be determined by the locale itself, however. Thus, strictly: a locale is incomplete if it contains a temporally outer tone x, inferior to another tone y of the locale by virtue of the relation constituting the locale . It does not effect the issue if there exists some other locale in which x is inferior to y. Note: The locales include all of Schenker's 'Zug's' but include other groups also; moreover, when counting a 'zug' as a locale, one must take care to exclude all tones which are irrelevant to the zug's being such. If this is not clear, the fault lies with the vagueness of 'zug' and not with 'locale' which is a precise term, as will be seen.

Winham here elaborates the heuristic rule that all such operations as the unprepared neighbor (that, in his phenomenology, would give rise to an unspecifiable proper memory span) need to be regarded as determining incomplete locales and thus must be subordinated to complete locales. The rule here is that operations are ordered by the need to conserve superiority (or the "Necessary" functions of particular tones): a tone may be inferior to another at one level only if this inferiority is determined by an incomplete locale (i.e., an unprepared neighbor or the like) that is incorporated into a complete locale (one that preserves a superiority of temporally outer tones).

After an intervening passage (that we will take up shortly), Winham further elaborates on the notion of analytic choice and the conservation of superiority, specifying that in problematic cases the "Necessary" function will be determined by simplicity of technique, or, as encountered earlier, the degree of change an operation causes on the operand: loosely, the series reads (in order of increasing complexity and decreasing change, and omitting octave shifting and purely artic- ulative operations): arpeggiation, passing motion, neighbor motion, suspension, and anticipation.

> 04(a). In certain cases one finds two functions of a tone, of which evi- dently at least one is Necessary, but not both. The decision as to which is the Necessary one is then made as follows: the types of locales are ordered as to simplicity-of-technique (though this order, again, is not a simple series); the simpler locale is then taken as the one determined by the Necessary function.
>
> (E.G., if a tone is both a lower neighbor to the third degree and also a passing tone in a 3-2-1, the 3 being the same one, the latter is taken as its Necessary function, on the grounds that the former demon- strates a more advanced technique in that it contradicts the tendency of the tone 2. The other function is not thereby denied, but counts as Unnecessary).
>
> 04(b). More rarely, this type of 'choice' may be between two func- tions which are mutually exclusive in that they offend the rule that x cannot be both superior and inferior to y in different locales (unless one is a subgroup of the other). In this case too the decision is based on which function demonstrates the simpler technique; and in this case the other one must be held not to exist at all. (The reason for this rule will emerge when we discuss examples.)

Following this, Winham moves to a prolongational protocol for the locale. The mechanics of prolongation, however, are not necessary to our point. As noted earlier, the predecessor to this theory assigned a level index to each tone. In terms of superiority–inferiority relations, the surface event with the lowest index would embody the longest chain of superiority relations. This new protocol grows obviously out of the need to legislate away some of the common problems that arose in the application of his previous protocol. But he makes one move that is more important than his attempt to define the mechanics of contain- ment relations. In this exposition, Winham abandons this notion of global level for logical reasons (as given in the intervening passage mentioned earlier):

> The concept of 'level' is rejected here because it is based on two con- ceptual confusions: 1. The idea that the superiority relation consti- tutes a series; 2. The idea that it is necessary or even possible to order the locales (or zugs) themselves as to Higher and Lower (or more-

or-less foreground or background), rather than the functions of their constituent tones.

One may still speak of levels-of-function of the single tone (if one remembers that not all of these levels are nicely arranged in series); but obviously this does not justify the practice of making a series of reductions of the whole piece and calling each successive one a higher level, a practice which is easily demonstrated to be arbitrary and misleading.

This rejection is justified at length in another passage [N22: 33–34].

In an analytic sketch it is necessary to distinguish various levels on which a given tone functions. If a tone X functions on a higher level than any on which a tone Y functions, X is *superior* to Y. The basic criteria are:

(1) a tone is inferior to another if it is dependent on it , in that it must lead to or from it according to a rule.
(2) a tone is inferior to another it if has a *tendency* to be followed or preceded by the other and in fact is, even if there is no *obligation* as in case (1).

These criteria are purely *local*, i.e., they give no means of distinguishing the levels of completely (temporally) separate motions. Hence there is no point in extracting everything "on a given level" in the sense of "any events of which none is superior to any other," and treating such a "level" as a unit. It follows that the word "level" is slightly misleading, as the hierarchy involved is not simply a succession of class-inclusions. Rather it is a "hierarchy" in the strict sense of Carnap, with the basic relation being class-inclusion. One may indeed give numbers to the levels in the sense: two motions are of the same level if they are n steps in the succession inferior to the "largest" motion; providing there is any *one* largest motion, which is not always the case. But even if it is the case, this numbering is insignificant for the reason already given, i.e., that events of a given level-number need have nothing else in common particularly.

This suggests the following more correct formal statement of the situation: Two events are *equal* if they are both superior to all the same events and inferior to all the same events. The important point is that *it does not follow* from the fact that neither of X and Y is *superior* to the other that they are equal. The latter case may be covered by the term *unordered*.

We may then reserve the term level for a class of all events which are equal to a given one. Derivatively, such classes may be subordinate to one another, or unordered. But no two such levels may be equal, or else they would merge into a single one.

This clears up the confusion resulting from the absence of clear criteria for what goes onto what "schicht" in Schenkerian analysis. We see that this confusion is not the result of any correctable failure to give such criteria, but of misunderstanding of the logical structure of the relation involved. When this is cleared up, the notion of a level as something picking out widely separated events from a context disappears, except in the case of the highest level, if there is one.

The definition of hierarchy as given by Carnap (that is found shortly after the part–whole system cited earlier) is fairly clear.[7]

> A relation H is called a *hierarchy* ('*Hier(H)*') provided the following three conditions obtain: *H* is asymmetric and one-many; *H* has exactly *one* initial member; and every member is only finitely many *H* steps removed from this initial member. The concept of hierarchy is related to that of progression (37a); the difference is that a progression is also many-one (hence one-one) and has no terminal member, whereas a hierarchy permits bifurcation in the direction away from the initial member and allows the occurrence of terminal members.

Carnap draws a distinction between a hierarchy and a progression (such as an ordered system of whole numbers generated, let us say, by the addition of a constant to an initial member, and the repeated addition of this same constant to the resultant sums). Winham draws a slightly different distinction between a hierarchy and a series (a progression with an initial and terminal member), but the point holds. He agrees with the classical Schenkerian that the textual analysis of a musical passage demonstrates the derivation of the musical surface through the recursive application of operations to a set of proper elements. (A more developed explication of hierarchical derivation will be presented shortly.) He makes the point, however, that absent a sort of "zero-level," it is impossible to render all the correct hierarchies manifested in the text commensurable. For example, one might reconstruct a passage in the beginning of a piece in terms of a five-step derivation, and likewise reconstruct a passage near the end of this same piece as a five-level derivation, yet it would be inaccurate to assume that the deepest levels in both analyses map corresponding or commensurable events.

---

[7]Carnap, *Introduction to Symbolic Logic and Its Applications*, 219.

In fact, the only way one can regard such events as 'ordered' is to presume a zero level that governs the entire piece. In this regard, though, Winham signals where he is going with this line of reasoning in two places in the penultimate quote above. In the second paragraph, he grudgingly admits the possibility of levels in the phrase "two motions are of the same level if they are n steps in the succession inferior to the largest motion; providing there is any *one* largest motion" but immediately adds "which is not always the case." In the concluding phrase of the quotation he more conclusively dismisses level "except in the case of the highest level," but again adds the qualification "if there is one." If there are to be 'levels', they can only arise given a global derivation of the piece, but Winham is skeptical about such a derivation.

In fact, though, he is more than skeptical about the plausibility of the Schenkerian *Ursatz*. In a remarkable collection of texts, he denies such a zero level on logical grounds. For example [*13a: 2]:

> Meanwhile, it is true that further research into the Schenkerian analytic method from this point of view has made it clear that the clarification of Schenker's 'techniques' by converting them into logical operations has certain limitations; the chief of which is that the distinguishing mark of the music to which this theory applies now appears to be not that the application of techniques (or any refinement of them) is demonstrable, but that it is demonstrable simultaneously in various apparently contradictory senses, i.e., that many opposed hierarchies of levels are to be found within the same works, but that the oppositions themselves are subject to explanation. Thus the reason 'Schenkerisation' of a piece by different analysts leads to different results is not only because the method is insufficiently clearly defined, but simply because the same result can be reached by different sequences of Schenker's operations; and the difference between a tonal and atonal piece of music is not that the latter cannot be produced from an Ursatz by Schenker's technique, but that the operations whereby the former is produced constitute an explanation having a certain simplicity (in that, for example, the same operations are successively used in successive levels, or that a given operation is *always* used whenever the operandum reaches a state with certain characteristics), whereas in the latter the procedure is chaotic.

Similarly, in relation to the rhythmic content of derivation [*13c: 4]:

> Perhaps the most critical defect of Schenker's theory lies in its rhythmic vagueness and hence its underrating of the importance of suspension and anticipation in the middleground. For this in turn led to

his failure to notice the essential ambiguity involved in these techniques, in that once they have been used, any further elaborating
notes have to be considered not only in relation to the *present* position
of the other tones, but also in relation to the *original* rhythmic position
of these tones, and this often creates quite different and interesting
progressions, etc.

On the other hand, once this systematic kind of ambiguity is recognized, it may be that the difficulty of arriving at well-defined grounds
for the uniqueness of a sketch-analysis will be greatly reduced. This is
not only because some of the different analyses are now subsumed
under one (or in other words, the ambiguity is blamed on the music,
not the method of analysis), but also because if every progression is
held to originate in a progression of equal-duration tones, before la-
beling some succession of tones a progression one has an additional
restricting obligation to show that some reasonable process of anticipating and delaying tones has produced the actual rhythm—reasonable in the sense that it is related to the other features of the context.

Asserted more formally in terms of the notion of tonal operations as containment relations [*3a: 2]:

The assumption hitherto shared by all analysts whose methods are in
any degree based on Schenker's theory, whether explicit or not, is that
the *containment relations* between tones or configurations of tones (e.g.,
triads) in a tonal piece are asymmetrical, as is containment in physical space. For example, if x is a neighbor to y, y allegedly cannot also
be a neighbor to x. To admit that *different analyses* of the same piece or
passage may have different merits and demerits, and that it is not necessarily the case that one is better than the other even if a criterion of
betterness is assumed, is not to challenge this assumption at all; for it
would remain to the point to ask whether these analyses actually con-
tradicted each other, and if it were concluded that they did, to main-
tain that one could not rationally assert them both simultaneously.

In detail [N19: 195]:

For a given piece, there may be infinitely many Schenkerisations. For
example, if there is an operation of 'erasure' whereby a tone on some
level is removed from the next, then evidently the same tone could be
erased and put back in see-saw fashion n times for any n, and there
would be at least one Schenkerisation for each n. But the same consequence follows from much less dubious operations. For example, if
there is an operation of octave transfer, then one may transfer the
same tone back and forth between the same two registers n times for

any n. Moreover, if same way could be found for reducing repetitions to single operations (which is not easy since other operations might intervene, etc.), one could still transfer a tone up n octaves for any n, one at a time, and then back again. Suppose that this is forbidden on the ground that the audible pitch range must not be exceeded, or some other ground. Then plenty of other ways of circumventing such prohibitions still exist. For example, given any tone, we can merely re-attack it half-way through its duration, and this process can be applied again to the first attack, and so on. But then *by virtue of a suspension of some previous tone in the same line*, all of these repetitions of attack can be wiped out. Thus anywhere that there is a suspension, we have infinitely many Schenkerisations according to how many times the absent portion of the resolving tone was subdivided. Perhaps, after all, some way of ruling out *all* such absurdities can be found. Certainly the problem is far from trivial. In the above case, for example, the reason why the subdivisions are forbidden seems to be that some *subsequent* operation is going to be applied. Here we may perhaps argue that this is not really so; what is incorrect is the suspension itself, on the ground that a suspension is forbidden to wipe out rhythmic distinctions. In other cases, it is not too clear that this argument will stand up.

and in sum [*16a: 1]:

It follows that "containment" relations are not necessarily asymmetrical and that there is no unique reduction in Schenker's sense; nevertheless there is a sequence of operations on a background which is unique to within minor differences (of order of operations). On the other hand, there is no reason in principle why a piece should not have two different backgrounds even in different keys, and this may be true of certain pieces. In that case there would be non-trivial differences and the idea of a unique series of sketches would be even more irrelevant.

Different Schenkerian analysts come up with conflicting analyses of the same text. The intuitive assumption is that this is a defect of the analytic system, one that can be remedied by a continuing program of refinement, remedied to the point at which it will become possible to determine the correct analysis. (As in the text about the different senses of the definition of tonal operations cited in the preceding section, such a process of remediation would involve adding conditions under which, for example, something would be said to be a 'neighbor' tone in, let us say, the 'middleground.') Winham's stipulation of hierarchies works around this problem. He takes the counterintuitive assumption that a systematic ambiguity is intrinsic to the music itself, and thus that competing analyses or hierarchies each capture some musical intuitions (and although some capture more than others all should be remarked).

A sense of this can be demonstrated through the examination of a simple passage. (This example, and the two succeeding, are of my devising. Lest it seem that I am placing too much of a burden on a "simple" passage, I would note that Winham, in a particularly striking moment of insight, gives as a general rule that "notable ambiguity arises in nonmodulations or small-range passages, rather than others. *The reason is that V, etc., have much the same scale.*" [S16: 2; a similar observation is also found at *25a: 4]).

Given an operational span encompassing only the last half of the first measure, the suspended C over G is inferior to (or displaced by) the succeeding B, yet given the entire passage, the tone B, as a neighbor, is inferior to the same C. In other words, the last portion of the initial C and B are governed by two containment relations each of which respectively reverses the other. Of course, this is a trivial example, and we can easily think of the larger operational span as in some way being hierarchically anterior to the smaller. Yet, the ambiguity here is without question part of the phenomenal content of the passage.

A second, slightly elaborated example gives more complexity to this line of reasoning.

The second B may be taken as a neighbor of C (and hence, despite its support, inferior). Unlike the first passing B, however, it is a more complex event. Indeed, if we read this second B not as a neighbor but as passing from A to the succeeding C, and thus assume it and its support to be rhythmically displaced from the third beat of the measure, it is superior to the preceding C:

Read this way, the initial C stands as an unprepared neighbor to B (unprepared because I assume that the initial B arises somewhat later in the derivation and that there is not symmetry of containment relations between it and C). Then again, it may stand beyond this as a remnant of a suppressed C governing all or part of the first measure, and thus superior to B (although this gives us some problems in reading B as passing from A to C. We might thus say that C is successively superior, inferior, and superior to B in this scenario.)

However, we could take the initial C (and the supporting G) as anticipating the C (and an implied G) in the second measure. Again, while C is inferior to B within the local context, it is superior within the complete locale. This anticipated C is different from the C that was a remnant of a C spanning the entire first measure. The two hierarchies, however, are different: one is a neighbor motion containing within it a passing motion, the second an arpeggiation containing a neighbor motion. But absent any other criteria (be it rhythmic, harmonic, or contextual) neither can be asserted as "more correct" than the other. The superiority relations between the first C and the second B remain the same: B is respectively inferior, superior, and inferior to C.

This situation becomes even more ambiguous when we involve derivations for each of these hierarchies. For the first hierarchy, such a derivation might read:

(1) An initial third on F moves to first inversion triad on E. (Inasmuch as this derivation is rhythmic, we are not adding pitches to sonorities by assuming shifting attacks.)

(2) A passing B bridges A and C, bisecting the first measure.

(3) The middle G of the second sonority is anticipated at the midpoint of the first sonority's span.

(4) The initial A is arpeggiated to C on the second beat of the first measure.

(5) This C is now suspended into the span of the neighbor B (giving, with the supporting G, a 4–3 suspension over F on the third and fourth beats).

(5) The first beat of the initial C is suppressed (what we had first described as an unprepared neighbor being truly an unprepared suspension).

(6) The final beat of the lower F and the initial beat of the anticipated G are suppressed.

(7) A passing B is added between the initial A and the suspended C.

(8) The middle G of the final sonority is suppressed.

A plausible derivation for the second hierarchy might read:

(1) A third moves to a first inversion triad (the upper voice by arpeggiation).

(2) The upper voices of the triad (G and C) are anticipated at the midpoint of the first measure and the second half of A suppressed.

(3) The anticipated C is given a neighboring B.

(4) The final beat of the lower F and the initial beat of the anticipated G are suppressed.

(5) A passing B is added between the initial A and the suspended C.

(6) The middle G of the final sonority is suppressed.

These two derivations prompt several points. First, while the second derivation seems "simpler," unfolding in six rather than eight steps, one cannot thus assert outright that it is more correct than the first (both, after all, preserving almost the same superiority relations: it might be argued that the relation between A and the first C changes, the former hierarchy reading it as the product of a later arpeggiation than the latter, but arpeggiation does not imply in itself a superiority relation). Second, even the number of steps in each hierarchy is open to question. Both derivations, for example, combine the suppressions of the last beat of F and of the initial beat of the anticipated G (at the middle of the first measure) in one step: these are unrelated operations, and one might say that they are unordered in respect to each other. (This in turn, though, obscures the fact that we might sense the F and G at some point as the beginning of a 3–2 suspension with F resolving to E: this interpretation would of course depend on whether F in a larger hierarchy functions as a passing tone, neighbor, or the like.) Consequently, there is no reason why both derivations could not be reordered to some extent.

Thus, Winham's notion of hierarchy becomes more complex. To speak of a particular hierarchy is, again, not to rule out the existence of other hierarchies. In fact, in many local or 'simple' passages the specification of one hierarchy is arbitrary. Further, the notion of 'number of steps in a derivation' is meaningless. This does not mean, however, that there are not criteria for evaluating hierarchies in these two respects, or that any hierarchy we might designate is equally valid. In both respects the analytic choice depends on the assumption of a hierarchy of operations, one in which there is not a strict order of power but a hierarchy itself of priority. Thus, Winham's taxonomy of operations comes into play, although in a fairly loose way. Arpeggiations take some priority over passing motions and neighbors, which in turn take priority to suspensions, which in turn are superior to purely articulative operations such as repetitions. Thus, the 'passing' hierarchy might be considered 'better' in some way than the 'anticipation' harmony by virtue of the relative priority of their initial operations. (This, though, merely constitutes a criteria for choice between analyses; a passing motion is not always superior to other motions, as is seen by the relegation of the first passing B to the last step of the derivation in both accounts.)

The function of the notion of hierarchy on the larger scale is similar (if paradoxically simpler). For any passage there are various hierarchies or derivations. To a certain extent, there are criteria for selecting the best such hierarchies. In fact, as passages get larger this discrimination becomes easier. There was one reading of the foregoing passage that was not noted. Winham, reading the discussion above, would ask why we do not even consider the possibility of the C in the opening measure functioning as a neighbor to the surrounding Bs. The answer of course is clear in this instance: the initial B is unsupported, and it would seem to suggest an unlikely hierarchy (i.e., the derivation of this hierarchy would start with a passing B bisecting the arpeggiation of A to C, and then anticipate this tone). Absent an explicit articulative indication evidencing such a hierarchy (such as a stress on the B), one would dismiss this reading. Yet, Winham would not let us off that easily: he would insist that even though this is in an obvious way a "deviant" hierarchy, it nonetheless is present as part of the phenomenal content of the passage, and therefore should be noted.

Given this account of Winham's conception of the analytic hierarchy, his dismissal of the *Ursatz*, and his postulation of a systemic ambiguity, we are equipped to further detail his implicit phenomenal construction of musical time. The first question that arises concerns the derivation of a real metric (i.e., one in which spans can be defined in terms of a real number of some base metric unit, even if that real number is, for example, the square root of two) from a rational metric. Returning to the derivations given above, and speaking in terms of a rational metric, the first derivation (1) bisects a span (i.e., locates a slice within the second span standing between the initial and end slices), (2) bisects the first section of this span, (3) bisects the first span of *this* span, (4) bisects the slice determined by (2) and then suppresses that slice, and (5) suppresses and then adds the slice determined by (3). The second derivation likewise creates a series of points or slices. Thus, even the simplest of passages contains (rationally) a whole series of initial slices (in any of its possible derivations) determined by layers of suppression and addition rather than simply those given at its surface. In a sense, the phenomena of pulse (and hence the ability to gauge "real" spans) arises out of a density of events within the domain of rational spans. This may be why the sense of a regular metric is lost as time span increases: the number of possible hierarchies decreases, and therefore each larger demarcation of time becomes somehow less dense.

But there is also a larger point to make, one that grows out of the notion of ambiguity and deviant hierarchies. The principal hierarchy in the following passage is obvious [*30ab; Pt. 2, IX: I expand on Winham's argument somewhat]:

There must be a passing motion from G to B at one level. The specifics of the derivation that determines this hierarchy are not completely clear: it may be that the passing A arises at the beginning of the third measure (and then is suppressed by a suspended G and reintroduced as a neighbor), and the resolving B is plausibly placed at its earliest point at the beginning of the fourth measure (and delayed by a lower-level passing A); or we might wish to place both originally in the fourth measure. What does seem clear is that the initial tone of the passing motion governs the first two measures and that the accented neighbor in the middle of the second measure is just that. Yet, the argument might be made that F♯ can be read not as a neighbor but as the initiating tone of a passing motion, and thus might determine an alternate hierarchy.

In this case, it is rather easy to dismiss this alternate hierarchy as deviant since it overlaps what must be a richer, truer hierarchy. But the choice between true and deviant hierarchies is not always so clear. For example, in one extended study [*16; Pt. 2, X] Winham examines the workings of such hierarchies in the opening of Beethoven's Op. 111, No. 2.:

He starts by noting the obvious harmonic reading of the first four measures as I–V–I–V. He then asks why this reading is preferable to one that takes the harmonic pattern of this phrase as V–I–I–V, the tonic upbeat suspended into the first measure, and the dominant suspended into the second. The ambiguity here turns on a reading of the bass C in the second measure. The first reading determines C as a passing tone resolving to D; the second makes it a resolution of the preceding B. The first is weakened by the enclosure of C within the previous first measure's D and B, the second by the enclosure of D by the third measure's E and C. The first reading, though, is preferable because the D in the second measure supports an alto F that must be a remnant of some proper element standing far back in the hierarchy as a member of the rising sixth that moves in the alto from E to G and in the soprano from C to E. Yet, the second reading (or deviant hierarchy it implies) cannot be dismissed, inasmuch as it is not clear which hierarchy predominates at the point of the bass C: the first reading of C only truly becomes "correct" when the sixths between alto and soprano become explicit in the third measure, while the second reading is supported by the earlier pattern of anticipations of I on the upbeat, of V in the first measure, and here again of I (although this pattern does conflict with the notion of an overall V–I–I–V).

Here, the notion of deviant hierarchies opens a dimension of the music that is lost in a more conventional analysis. The flexibility of his analysis, and his sensitivities to weightings and shadings in the text are born from the notion of systematic ambiguity. I think though, that this ambiguity is tied closely to the precision of his theory.

Winham gives us two very different sorts of musical explication. On the one hand, he puts forward a set of analytic guidelines that assume hierarchies of time–pitch spans implying but not specifying a serial order of derivation (and themselves dependent on a hierarchy of priorities of operations), and that only loosely distinguish among true and deviant hierarchies (the presence of a global hierarchy being desirable in this regard but misleading). On the other hand, he gives a phenomenology of music constructed axiomatically (at least in potential) from minimal premises (such as "earlier-than," "higher in pitch," "similar to the overtone series," or "similar to the unordered set of memory spans"). There is a system of balances holding between these two modes of explication: a balance between the specific and the general, and between the heuristic and axiomatic.

Most important, though, there is a balance that holds between degrees of certainty, one best explicated by returning to Winham's conception of a matrix of logical problems (i.e., the distinction between analysis and synthesis, the definition of the musical score and musical work, and the specification of musical structure). The point of his clarification of the difference between description and analysis is that even what seems a descriptive statement (for example, "work W begins and ends on the same pitch") has an analytical content: in fact, the only true descriptive statement would be one that confined itself to the physical characteristics of events (for example, "the first note of work W is middle C and the last note of work W is middle C"). Two paths lead from this distinction. Winham follows, on the one hand, the notion of a minimal relation, one whose characteristics can be fixed with a degree of certainty. The relation "same-pitch" has a phenomenal reality and thus can be given as a primitive in a formal language of music. The virtues of such choice include the fact that such a primitive could not be said to be arbitrary and that a musical structure (in the sense that such relations can be qualitatively described as "symmetrical," "transitive," or the like) can be elaborated, which is likewise not arbitrary. Expanded, such a language could incorporate such phenomenological qualities of music as temporal and pitch asymmetries, particularly in so much as they define the musical work. As a phenomenological language, though, it is always by comparison with the physical description of the musical object "analytic." On the other hand, the second path is that of analysis per se, that which extrapolates directly from the score (a description) and discerns musical structures (tonal operations, hierarchies of inclusion, and the like). Given that the relation "inferior within an operation" holding between tones cannot be defined (because the operation itself cannot be conclusively defined), and given that it is not necessarily structurally invariant (in that two tones may reverse their superiority relations in reference to two different operations), such relation is to a great degree arbitrary. This is not to say that the specification of superiority relations and the hierarchies they determine are not valuable, but to assert a distinction between different sorts of musical significance, or different strengths of claims to significance.

One suspects that at some point Winham presumed that a formal language of music would provide a criteria with which to strengthen the claims of this second analysis, and thus his project remained incomplete. (I would say *strengthen* rather than *give certainty to* because Winham always distinguishes between a sort of *a priori* significance and a significance of context.) But I think that he arrives at a more nuanced and powerful conception, in that he comes to value the discipline of holding to distinct levels of musical significance and in that even if his axiomatic "language" for music remains unfinished, his work as a whole reaches a certain closure.

Although his phenomenology does not directly or demonstrably connect with his analytic practice, it without question informs that practice. In effect, the systematic definition of his phenomenal construction is tied to the systematic ambiguity of his analysis. Ruling out the arbitrary choice of axioms and primitives in his language of music, he likewise rules out the notion of an axiomatic reconstruction of Schenker as a set of operations on an arbitrary primitive (i.e., the *Ursatz*). The somewhat ambiguous notion of hierarchy (and in this we include the notion of deviant hierarchies) is plausible as a means of expressing a partial representation of the infinite set of proper memory spans, whereas the notion of levels and strict derivations is not.

Thus, Winham's theoretical constructions and his analytical guidelines balance each other in a sort of epistemological suspension. It is out of this suspension that he brings under examination a density of musical experience and intuitions.

PART 2:

Selected Excerpts

I.

*37a: 2–7

I think that this passage is Winham's most complete discussion
of the distinction between descriptive and explanatory or analytic statements. As such, it returns to a ground that Winham previously has covered on several occasions, yet goes further than the others, touching on
such points as the choice of axioms for a theoretical system and the like.
(Of particular interest is the reference to Allen Forte and the free choice
of axioms.) As is sometimes the case, in the original Winham misdesig-
nates the third footnote as "1," something that I have corrected.

Description and analysis

1. It now seems to me that a perfectly clear-cut distinction between
descriptive and analytic[1] statements about music can be rigorously
formulated. The difference is one of meaning, not form, in the sense
that a purely descriptive statement is such that not only can it never
be rephrased as an analytic statement, but that no analytic statement
can be deduced from it. This is therefore a non-trivial and important
distinction.

2. It is not to be expected, nevertheless, that given any statement of
the usual sort, our definitions will enable us to immediately decide
whether it is analytic or not. This is because of the vagueness of many
such statements. One may have to ask the author certain questions in
order to determine more precisely the sense of his statement as intended. However, these questions are quite clear, and I think that a de-

---

[1] 'Analytic statement' here means, of course, 'statement analyzing the form of
a piece of music;' it has nothing to do with the logical sense of 'analytic,' i.e., 'true by
virtue of meaning.' This is an unfortunate coincidence.

cision can be arrived at in all cases. Assuming the author grasps elementary logic (in a purely common-sense way), these questions would be of the form "From your statement, do you intend that . . . should logically follow, or not?", etc. Thus only his meaning in the sense of deductive consequences, not in the sense of semantical designation, is in question. This is one reason that the matter turns out to be surprisingly clear and definite.

3. The difficulty of distinguishing between descriptive and analytic statements seems to arise thus: given a descriptive statement, a rewording of it seems to result in an analytic statement, even though it seems obvious that the latter is logically equivalent to or weaker than the former. Hence, it seems the distinction must be purely verbal and of no interest. Now I shall argue that what really happens is this: the rewording only *seems* to be equivalent or weaker, when read literally; but actually a claim has crept in unnoticed through the connotations of the new words. We recognize this claim when we intuitively feel that the statement is analytic; but then when we recompare it with the former statement to determine their logical relationship, we return to the more literal reading and thus fall victim to equivocation. Let us analyze this process in detail with an example. As two obviously purely descriptive statements, take the following:

(A) "The work W begins with middle C"
(B) "The work W ends with middle C"

Now if our distinction is to be nontrivial, the conjunction of these two must remain purely descriptive, as we would indeed judge it to be. But now consider the statement:

(C) "The work W begins and ends with the same pitch"

This is obviously an analytic statement. Yet it seems to be logically actually weaker than the conjunction of (A) and (B), since together they imply it but the converse does not hold. Thus our distinction seems to evaporate into being purely verbal.

Now this is my contention: When comparing (C) with (A and B) we read it in a quite literal sense, expunging all intuitive feelings about its connotations in order to exactly measure its logical force. What we overlook is a claim, beyond this sense, which is subtly implied in the phraseology, or rather, in this case, two such claims. These are that:

(1) There is an a priori significance in the relationship between beginnings and ends, by virtue of their positional isomorphism with respect to a qualitative order, here the temporal order. That this is a non-

tautological claim is evident from the crucial word 'qualitative.' Any two events are positionally isomorphic to some order or other. 'Qualitative' or some related term such as 'similar' must be taken as primitive. That the temporal order has a name is a hint that it is qualitative, but certainly no proof of it, since we can give a name to any order we choose.

(2) Sameness of pitch is, likewise, a qualitative or "given" relation. This is subtly implied by the very word "same". Again, the claim cannot be made trivial by logical characterization of the relation as an equivalence relation (transitive and symmetrical); because any two events stand in infinitely many such relations. The claim here gets overlooked chiefly because its truth is so obvious. But this truth, again, is by no means established by the identity of name ('middle C'); for we may invent names to cover all and only any events we wish.

Hence statement (C) implies that two such qualitative classes have the same extension among events in the work W. This is what makes it analytic.[2]

I hope that the situation is now quite clear. The statement (C), which looks weaker than (A and B), is actually, in its intended sense, much stronger. Moreover, it is stronger in a specific way: it makes claims as to the empirical givenness, qualitativeness, significance or whatever one may wish to call it, of some properties and relations of musical events as opposed to others. Just what these claims amount to (they are probably matters of degree) awaits precise explication which is not possible here. In any case, for reasons too complex to go into here, I am convinced that at least one such predicate must be taken as an ultimate primitive, and certain statements as to what kinds of events satisfy it as axioms, in addition to the descriptive characterization of the work, in order to deduce analytic statements.

4. The necessity for assuming such axioms does not, of course, mean that we can take any axioms we choose. This fallacy has been much defended lately, especially by Allen Forte. This is true only in the sense that we can, in a free country, say anything we like. What is fallacious is the implication that there is no truth-criterion for such statements. Pursued to its logical conclusion, this would mean that to at-

---

[2] Perhaps claim (1) is already hinted at by the conjunction (A and B). But both (1) and (2) are necessary to make an analytic point, for obvious reasons (which will be explicitly formulated at the end of this paper).

tribute similarity to events of the same pitch has no better justification than attributing it to any arbitrary class of events. A further inescapable consequence is that any two works containing the same number of events would be such that any analysis of one of them could be rephrased as an analysis of the other and be equally valid. For obvious reasons, this amounts to the identity, as far as analysis is concerned, of all works with each other. (The fallacy seems, in Mr. Forte's writing, to arise out of a commendable effort to make all his assumptions explicit, combined with two confusions: (a) between phenomenally given relations, and associations generated by musical contexts; and (b) between assumptions of the analyst and "assumptions of the work" itself in a mysterious sense.) This truth-criterion ultimately resides in psycho-acoustics. In most cases there is no disagreement, though there are borderline cases such as the question of octave-association. Hence the proper method for the musical analyst seems to be to state his axioms not as arbitrary postulates but as serious claims; and to leave their substantiation to others, it being outside his field.

5. Now let us retrace our steps and clearly formulate the description-analysis distinction, having shown how it comes to be obscured. For this purpose we have to suppose that all the statements we are concerned with have been clarified as to their deductive consequences; and that we have constructed, for a given work, a sufficient set of axioms concerning the qualitativeness of properties and relations exemplified by its events. We will call this set of axioms S. We also of course presuppose a logical linguistic framework L, including a theory of classes in some form. To say that P can be deduced from q then means that P becomes a theorem if q is added to the axioms of this framework. Finally, we presuppose a sufficient description D, a set of statements such that *just one work can exemplify all of them*. The criterion for this is of course simply the laws of sound-phenomena, such as that a minimal event cannot be both higher and lower than another, must have one and only one pitch, etc. It is not necessary that the statements of D be independent of one another or in any way prevented from irrelevance. But we ensure that nothing about qualitativeness slips in here by requiring that *each primitive predicate apply only to events or ordered n-tuple of events, not to classes or attributes of them*. A descriptive statement, then, is simply one employing only first level primitives and terms defined exclusively in terms of first-level primitives. Not all such statements will be relevant, but this is of no concern for our purpose.

Now an analytic statement is, according to my explication, *one which can be deduced from S and D together, but not from either S or D alone.*

Going back to our examples A, B, and C, it is easily seen that A and B can be deduced from D alone. But C, if understood as making the claims I suggested, cannot be deduced from either S or D separately, but can be deduced from both together.

6. Finally, we can give a criterion for the truth or falsity of an analytic statement. Clearly, if S contains a false axiom necessary to deduce P, P must be false. But if the axioms of S are all true and P follows from them, P must be true (the question of whether D is true of course does not arise, since this is just a matter of what work we are talking about). And the truth of S we have already delegated to be settled by psycho-acoustics. For the purpose of our field, then, S must be the final court of appeal. In this sense, then we can say that an analytic statement is "true" if it satisfies the general condition for an analytic statement given above; and we could call a statement "analytically false" if its negation can be deduced from S and D. Just how we decide to use the terms "true" and "false" here is not important, provided we use them only one way at a time and make clear which sense is meant. The first of these suggested senses makes "true" mean "empirically true," i.e., corresponds to the fundamental normal sense of the word; whereas the latter is essentially short for something like "true if the axioms of musical analysis are true." This sort of transferred usage is not uncommon, especially in mathematics. Personally, I think there are good pragmatic reasons to object to it. But it is useful as a means of drawing a firm line between fields—in this case, of not having to bring psycho-acoustics into every musical discussion.

II.

N19: 31–34

This passage engages at length the distinction between physical events and phenomenal events. Of particular interest is the rejection of sense-data as a criterion for determining if something is "phenomenal."

Now for example, when a musical performance takes place, and various people hear it, they each perceive a sequence of events which is a sequence of phenomena. These sequences of phenomena have different properties; for example, if one person is sitting nearer the sound-source than another, his phenomena may be louder or have different timbres, etc. It is possible that among the phenomena "of" one person, there may be some for which *no* corresponding ones occur in the experience of some other persons; e.g., the other may be too far away to hear a certain very soft tone at all, or he may have a physical defect in his ear. However, it also may be the case that the corresponding phenomenon *did* occur in his experience, but he didn't *notice* it because at that moment he was attending to another voice, etc. Similarly, one person might hear one tone *as* higher than another, while the other person heard two corresponding tones which he did not compare as to height, perhaps because they were of different timbres, etc.; and in such a case (if we are talking about phenomena and not sense-data) we would usually (barring special circumstances of his physique or where he was in the room, etc.) assert that his phenomena nevertheless had this relation, though he didn't notice it.

If we examine the various theories of hearing or of 'psycho-physical' acoustics, etc., etc., we can quickly be assured that whether they know or admit it or not, these theorists use the concept of phenomena almost invariably, as opposed to sense-data. This can easily be seen from the following example: it is asserted, say, that pitch is determined by or correlated with frequency (that this oversimplified theory is only approximately true is beside the point here), by the law that the ratio of frequencies equals the difference of pitches. Now if this were intended to correlate *sense-data* with physical events, it would clearly be refuted by millions of counter-examples every minute of every day, namely every time someone listens to a tune and doesn't notice anything about it except that it sounds pretty, etc.; and the same goes for about every assertion of psycho-acoustics.

Another example is the simple statement that concert A equals 440 vibrations per second. This, if meant as asserting A for the property of sense-datum of being concert A, would (apart from the above problem about noticing), be true only for people with absolute pitch; for the rest of us *there is no such property* of our sense-data as being concert A. Thus the statement is obviously intended to refer to phenomena, not sense-data. (Concert A = 440 for the rest of us too, only we aren't able to tell this directly, but have to rely on those with absolute pitch for this assurance).

At this point we may already perhaps somewhat clarify the sense in which it is reasonable to demand that musical analysis "refer to the ear" etc., without either (a) meaning that it must be based on physiological as well as musical evidence or (b) begging the question of whose ear and under what circumstances. Namely, it is reasonable to demand that musical analysis speak, ultimately, though perhaps highly indirectly, about properties of phenomena rather than of physical objects such as ink spots on paper, or physical events such as expansion of air molecules or electrical currents or contact between fingers and pieces of ivory. Later we will be able to be more specific about this, i.e., we will offer a suggestion as to just *what* statements about phenomena are statements of musical analysis.

In approaching this problem, we may observe that a conspicuous property of musical analysis is that it is analysis *of* something, namely a musical work. Thus at least one of its sources of confirmation or evidence must be that work; if we know something about what counts as evidence for or against some assertion, we know something about the assertion, and in this case perhaps the main thing we want to know about it; therefore it will help to first decide just what a particular musical work is, since there seems to be some doubt and disagreement on this point.

In answering this question, we are *explicating* the common-sense notion of "musical work", and so it must be understood that this explication does not have a truth-value, but only a degree of clarity, relevance, and fruitfulness as compared with other explications. By clarity here we mean the degree of agreement obtainable as to whether something is or is not an instance of the explicatum. For example, the explication of the explicatum "musical work" by the concept "succession of tones" would pass this test, but that by the concept "unified musical whole" would not. By relevance we mean degree of coextensiveness with the explicandum, whose vagueness prevents exact coextension. For example, "musical score" would fail this test because in that case there would be thousands of Beethoven's-fifth-symphonies instead of only one. But "set of equivalent musical scores" would pass this test fairly well, except for such facts as these: In saying that a work is "long" we are unlikely to be speaking of the length of equivalent scores, since these may be all different sizes depending on how large is the print, etc. However, the real difficulty with this explication is that it is useless *unless we have a definition* of 'equivalence', but such a definition clearly must be given in terms of *description or prescription of the same sound* (in some sense), and this would be to admit what is in any case obvious, namely that scores are descriptions or prescriptions of something else; and the customary usage of "musical work" is clearly very far from suggesting that such an entity is a description or prescription of something else. And even if we were to decide that nevertheless it actually is such an entity, we would have only pushed our problem a stage further back, as now we must find out what kind of entity it is that a musical work describes or prescribes. By fruitfulness we mean the stability of generalizations or laws involving the explicatum, i.e., whether it is worthwhile to use such a concept, regardless of whether it is relevant to this or any common sense term. On this count all the above-mentioned explanations trivially pass, because they are well-known, well-used terms already; this count is applied to deciding between new terms.

We have of course already suggested what our explication will be by (1) accepting as reasonable the demand that analysis be 'aural' and (2) explicating that as meaning 'referring to phenomena', and (3) observing that analysis is of works. It would follow that works should be phenomena or sets or some other abstraction from phenomena. Specifically, we suggest that a musical work is *that set of successions of phenomena which satisfy the description or prescription contained in some score or other similar specification.*

III.

*79u: 3–6

This is the single passage where Winham explores at length the phenomenal basis for an axiom system for timbre and sketches out such a system. The references are to Nelson Goodman's *The Structure of Appearance* (Cambridge, Mass.: Harvard University Press, 1951). There is a lacuna between the fifth and sixth paragraphs that is indicated here by a space.

Thus for normal orchestral works we can probably get along with about four primitives, having to do with 1) degrees of similarity in respect of basic color-characteristic, 2) degree of similarity in respect to brightness, 3) in respect to clarity, 4) degree of mixture.

Those readers with a feeling for the aesthetics of logical construction will, however, be unpleased with the prospect of a battery of four-place primitives. So we must now consider whether we can either 1) reduce each to a primitive of fewer places, or 2) reduce them all to fewer terms, preferably one. An analogous problem is dealt with by Goodman[3], who considers a four-term predicate of color-similarity, and rejects it in favor of a two-term predicate for matching colors which are different but not discriminably so (so that the predicate is not transitive). However, in order to generate an order from this, he

---

[3] Goodman, pp. 220 ff.

has to make the assumption that "given any two qualia belonging to the same category (i.e., colors, places, etc.) we can trace a path from one to the other by a series of steps, each to a quale matching the preceding one".[4] This *may* be true, but it seems to me hardly sufficiently obvious to justify basing the color-order on it. In any case, we cannot make any such assumption if the domain is limited to a single musical system, since in that case it is clearly false. On the other hand, in such a limited domain there is no objection to taking as a primitive the relation of least-discernible difference, of which the lesser degrees of similarity are then powers.

The interesting cases are those where a new color is heard, but at the same time the components are discriminable. This can even arise if the component tones are not at the same pitch, but phenomena of that sort are far too complex for us to have any hope of dealing with them systematically.[5]

Consider the simple case such as a viola and a clarinet playing (simultaneously) the same pitch. They are discernible as such, but there is also a total color of their sum. This is what some psychologists call an "emergent" quality, but having a name for it does not get us anywhere. Again, the problem is to describe this in a way that brings out its structural significance. We cannot simply define this color as the color which a sum-individual has if its component individuals have the colors VA and CL, and are simultaneous and of the same dynamic, or something of the sort; because some colors do not mix in this way, and we must have some way of distinguishing the "emergent" color-terms from those which are simply defined by simultaneity of the other colors. Also, introducing these mixed colors as primitive predicates is useless, since if they are formally equivalent to some combination, *within the system* it will make no difference that they are not defined in terms of that combination. So we must hunt around for some device analogous to that of defining the atomic colors in terms of degrees of similarity.

The first point to note is that to what extent tones mix is, of course, a function of their pitch, time and dynamic qualities (and perhaps even of their degrees of attack-distinctiveness). Thus, for example, the formal equivalence of the relation "mix to the maximum degree" to some other predicate will not be trivial. We might therefore again take

---

[4] Goodman, pp. 223. The fact that Goodman's atoms are quale and not minimal events clearly does not destroy the analogy in the problem.

[5] Except that we might to try deal with the cases where the two tones are an octave apart (or a multiple of an octave).

a primitive four-term relation "x mixes with y more than z does with u". Note that the maximum degree of mixture is not indiscriminability of components, since in that case there is only one individual involved. Alternatively, however, we could suppose that every x mixes with itself to the maximum degree, and that no two different tones

Suppose a work uses n different atomic colors, and that the only relevant way of classifying these is into K different groups, each of which may have subgroups. For example, a work for VN, VA, VC, DB, FL, OB, CL, BN, TPT, HN, TRB, TBA has 12 atomic colors, divisible into 2 groups (four STR versus eight W) of which the second is further divisible into 2 groups of four (WW vs. BR). Thus S^1xy means that x and y have the same atomic color. S^2xy means they are within one of the groups STR, WW, BR. S^3 means they are within the group W, and S^4 that one is STR and the other W. This scheme can be generated by a four-term relation: x is more similar to y than z is to u. In this manner only the structure, and every relevant aspect of the structure, is revealed (one could of course further subdivide the groups, but I am assuming this is not relevant). To show what this means, the "significant" predicate STR, for which STR $=$(V v VA v VC v DB) holds, is distinguishable from the "insignificant" predicate A, defined thus: A $=$ (VN v BN v TPT v TBA), by the fact that any pair of which STR is true of both will be at least similar to degree S^2, whereas the same does not hold for A. This structure of the color scheme would not be revealed if the twelve atomic colors were taken as primitive terms, and the groups defined by them; in that case, STR and A would be in no sense a priori distinguished.

Now if there is more than one way of classifying the colors (e.g., if tonal brightness is taken into account), we simply use another primitive four-place relation; so this creates no problem. More interesting is the question of mixture of colors. Of course if this merely produces a new color, and is not in any audible sense a compound, we simply include the new color in the basic scheme. There is a distinction of clarity between unmixed and mixed colors even if we cannot distinguish the components of the latter, but this can be taken care of by another primitive relation.

The trouble is that this does not do the job. For example, to say that a tone which is VN bears relation S^2 to one which is OB is not to say that there is a third tone to which the first bears S^1 and which bears S^1 to the second.[6] Indeed, this is clearly false in a limited domain, and may well be false in general, no matter what degree of difference S^1 is

---

[6] In other words, we cannot identify these superscripts with the usual notation for relation-powers.

intended to mean. In other words, contrary to Goodman's assumption it may be that categories of quale are not orderable by means of any one two-term relation in this sort of manner. *Some* such categories undoubtedly are; but to assume that *all* are is a much stronger assertion than Goodman seems to realize. Another way of putting it is to note the danger of confusion between degrees of similarity and powers of a relation of similarity-to-a-given-degree.

Now one might be inclined to give up the task of reducing the primitive four term-relation as hopeless, on the epistemological (or psychological?) ground that it is by comparing *pairs* of data that we acquire the notion of degree of similarity. But even if this is true, it does not follow that a reduction must be impossible. All that is necessary is that in the reducing we avoid assuming dubious hypotheses.

IV.

*14b

Winham's phenomenal construction of harmonic events evolves through the course of several manuscripts. Perhaps the most interesting is *14b, which gives a set of axioms (no axioms are found in *1e, the text explicated in my essay) and a number of definitions not found elsewhere: it is these axioms and additional definitions that are given here. In regard to the first, I think that each of these "axioms" could be developed as a theorem in his later system. *14b is, like *1e, made up of single sheets, each of which at the top contains several lines. Unlike *1e, several of the definitions are repeated and sharpened on succeeding sheets. Also unlike *1e, these sheets were not numbered by Winham himself, but rather by the editor as found: I will put these editorial numbers in brackets after the definitions.

A. There exist scales associated with fundamental-chords of order 3, but not with fundamental chords of lower order than 3. [2]

A. Each diatonic-scale has tonics belonging to just two PCs. [13]

A. (Uniqueness of root) If x is a root of some chord, another tone in the chord is a root of it if and only if it belongs to the same PC as x. [16]

A. (Consistency of dichordal consonance with temperament) x is consonant if and only if it belongs to a primary chord. [19]

A. (Dissectiveness of consonance) If x is consonant, every part of x is consonant. [20]

A. There exist chords which are not consonant though all their constituent dichords are consonances. [21]

A. (Consistency of scale association with temperament) Each diatonic-scale is associated with a complete basic chord. [23]

A. (Uniqueness of gamut) There is exactly one gamut containing a given pitch, and it has 12 PCs. [25]

A. (Exhaustive assignment of roots to consonant chords) A chord is consonant if and only if it has a root. [26]

A. The bass of a basic chord is a root of it if and only if it is primary. [27]

A. (Uniqueness of association, (2)) There is exactly one scale associated with a given complete basic chord. [28]

x and y differ at least by z: x and y differ by some z_1 such that z is intervalically equal to or smaller in pitch span than z_1. [3]

x is a minimal integral chord: x is an integral chord such that no octave-similar integral chord is smaller in pitch span. [4]

x is a diatonic-total: for every segment of some fundamental scale y there is a segment of x which is a tempered-representation of y. [14]

x is a consonance: x is a tempered representation of a concordance. [17]

x is a complete basic chord: x is a basic chord such that for any y belonging to a pc not occurring in x, (x + y) is not a basic chord. [22]

x is a comma: if y and z are segments of the same fundamental-scale containing the same number of pitches but are not intervalically equal, they differ at least by x. [33]

x is a comma-free representation of y: x has the same number of pitches as y; for any dichords x_1 and x_2 which respectively correspond in x to y_1 and y_2 in y, x_1 and x_2 are intervalically equal if and only if y_1 and y_2 differ at most by a comma; otherwise x_1 is smaller in pitch-span than x_2 if and only if y_1 is smaller in pitch-span than y_2. [34]

x differs from y by more than x_1 does: z and z_1 exist such that z_1 is smaller in pitch-span than z; x differs from y by z, and x_1 differs from y by z_1. [38]

x exceeds y by z: there is some x_1 which lies between parts of x in pitch, such that for some x_2 which outlines (x + x_1), a part x_3 of x_2 exists such that (x + x_3) is intervalically equal to y; another part x_4 of x_2

exists, such that x_4 is not equal in pitch to x_3, and such that $(x_1 + x)$ is intervallically equal to z. [39]

x is more fundamental than y: x is a fundamental chord of order n, where y is not a fundamental chord of order $\leq$ n. [43]

x is a quasi-direct-root of y: y is not a basic harmony, but all the dichordal parts of y are consonances and at least one is a basic dyad; x is a part of y which belongs to the same pc as the direct root of any most basic dyad of y. [45]

x and y are in the same position: every dichord in x containing a bass of x is diatonically octave-equivalent to a dichord in y containing y's bass, and vice versa. [50]

V.

*13c

This passage is a rather informal (and preliminary) attempt to construct a usable taxonomy of techniques or tonal operations. It is found in a manuscript grouping (*13) that is thematically consistent in its focus on the tonal operations. The particular subgrouping of which it is a part (*13c) begins with a discussion of the problematic place of arpeggiation within a system of tonal operations, and then elaborates on two theories of these operations, of which this is the second (and more complete). Note the way in which arpeggiation is here developed as a derived technique. (To be consistent, I think that Winham, as indicated on an earlier page, would think of both anticipation and suspension as derived techniques, and that he would certainly clarify (6).) Note also in (7) the rationale for considering the neighbor motion to be more primitive than the passing motion.

(1) Coupling

This is merely the addition of another representation of the same PC, simultaneous with the origin and identical in duration. It is in a sense the most primitive of all techniques, based merely on octave-association and no other assumption.

(2) Generation of triad

The third or fifth above the given tone may be added in the same way as coupling.

Note: By combination of (1) and (2) the fourth below, etc., may also be added. This does *not* mean that every triad in a piece is regarded as originating in root position, since we will give other ways of arriving at non-root position triads. However, it does mean that any tone with a purely *harmonic* origin derives from this process (this will be explained below).

Restriction on (2). Triad-generation can be applied only to tones *not* themselves generated in this way. (This restriction prevents building up in thirds of fifths to seventh-chords, ninth chords, etc.; the seventh, ninth, etc. must be derived linearly—(see below).

(3) Subdivision

This consists of the division of the duration of the tone into a *prime number* of *equal segments*, with a reattack at each join.

Notes: 1. The restriction to primes is ineffectual in preventing non-prime subdivisions, of course, since they are obtained by repeated application of the same technique. But this restriction leads to a *measurability of the number of applications* required to reach a given subdivision. 2. The restriction to equal segments, on the other hand, is highly constraining. The point of this is that unequal segments have to be regarded as resulting from rhythmic displacement (see below). 3. Instead of a subdivision technique, a repetition technique could be defined, but this is more complicated (for example, it extends one tone beyond the end of others; also the restriction on unequal subdivision is not easy to translate into the required form).

(4) Suppression

This consists of simply omitting a tone. But there is a very important restriction: A tone must not be omitted unless either (a) techniques (1) or (3) have been applied to it (so that it still has a representative in a sense) or (b) it originated through the application of technique (1) or (3), and (4) is *not* applied to its origin (for the same reason) or (c) it originated through technique (2) *and* had some technique applied to it (in order that it is both possible and necessary (respectively) to invoke this tone's presence at some stage, as being "defined by the harmony").

Note 1: Derived Technique—arpeggio.

This is accomplished as follows: First, by (2), a harmonic interval is generated. Then by (3), both tones are subdivided into 2 (for example). Finally, by (4), the first of one pitch and the second of the other are suppressed. This leaves the harmonic interval in linear form. (This sounds rather laborious, but actually only spells out precisely what is usually meant by "breaking a chord"—the important point is that arpeggiation originates in simultaneity, or else there is no difference between this and step-motion).

(5) Merger

This is the converse of subdivision, i.e., any configuration of a prime number of equal-duration attacks of the same pitch may be reduced to one tone. The point of it is that in this way unequal durations are produced. E. G., if ♩ is subdivided into ♪♪ and then ♫♫ one may then merge the first *three* only, yielding ♪.♪ .

Note: This could also be regarded as a variant of technique (4) except that only *attacks* are suppressed.

But there is a slight difference: ♪♫ cannot be reduced to ♪.♪ by merger, because of the inequality of the first two durations. In order to admit this case, one has to invoke attack-suppression.

(6) Tie, Anticipation

When a tone has been subdivided and the original suppressed, a previous tone may be held through the rest. Similarly, if the new tone is suppressed, a following tone may be extended backwards to cover the rest.

However, similar extensions may take place without any specific rest to cover.

Note: Ambiguity. Different techniques lead sometimes to the same result. In such cases there is not necessarily any need to decide which is responsible. But on the contrary, it is important to observe that *both* may be relevant. For example, ♪.♪ may arise by (5), or by (6). On the other hand, often one or the other will be obviously more relevant. This creates a problem of analysis, but should not create any problem with regard to description, which may be satisfied by showing that at least one technique has generated a given situation.

(7) Elaboration and Connection

This is the filling of a rest created by suppression with neighbor or passing tones, respectively. Note that the former is more primitive in the sense that it can exist without triad-generation, whereas the latter cannot. In fact, the latter presupposes arpeggiation.

(8) Alteration

This is the replacement of one tone by another which is a semitone away.

Note: The difference between 'chromatic alteration' and 'mixture' is only that the latter does not introduce a new tonicization, but only a new modality. (It seems misleading to regard them as entirely separate notions as does Schenker.)

The circumstances under which this is reasonably invokable are obviously quite limited, but no absolute rule seems called for (E.G., a double alteration, though peculiar, is not unthinkable; and 'resolution' by step does not always take place, though usually it does since the tonicization was the whole point of introducing the change).

VI.

N19: 195–200

This text asserts the impossibility of a noncontextual definition of the tonal operation and the notion of relative adequacy of analyses. In the manuscript, there are two brief passages that seem to have nothing in particular to do with this line of reasoning, so I have omitted them (while noting the presence of intervening material).

1. Let us assume that all the categories of the tonal system are *defined* by a specification of the *minimal necessary* conditions under which one might conceivably invoke them. Thus for example 'y passes from x to z' is to mean 'x, y and z are in that time order and (x,y) and (y,z) are step-classes whose generating steps are in the same direction' or something of the sort. To distinguish this sense of 'passes' and analogous senses of 'arppeg. of' etc., from any other senses, we may use subscripts '1,' thus: 'passes$_1$,' etc.

2. Notice that not all of the terms are easy to define even in this minimal sense. For example 'y is a passing tone$_1$' might be true even if there is no z such that for some x, y passes from x to z; as in the case of a V^7 followed by an octave-tonic with no third, at the end of a piece. In view of cases like this we seem forced to the conclusion that 'is a passing tone$_1$' applies to every tone. This may not be so bad as it sounds, since it does not prevent us from denying that for a given x and z, y passes from x to z.

3. Now it might seem that all these terms with subscripts '1' would be so trivial as to be useless. But this need not be so for more complex terms which we can define in terms of basic ones. For example, consider the term 'P_1' defined thus: 'x, y and z stand in the relation P_1 if and only if y passes from x to z in register, and there is no u (such that

u $\neq$ z) which also passes from x to z, and x and z are each respectively simultaneous with some PC-equivalents of one another, and (the duration x - to - z) = (the duration y - to - z)'.

Similarly, in such a manner we could define the relations of '*level-subordination*' or '*containment of motions*.' First of all in analogous fashion to 'passes$_1$.' Then certain more complex relations which are sub-relations of these could be given, just as P_1 is a sub-relation of 'passes$_1$.'

4. It is an interesting question whether everything to which one would really wish to commit oneself in Schenkerising a piece could be expressed by means of this kind of terminology. It would certainly be a greatly desirable situation if one could, for there is nothing to prevent the "Subscript-'1' language" from being absolutely precise and subject to rigid proof-criteria, etc.

Actually, I think, this program would fail. However, I think that nevertheless the "Subscript-'1' language" is useful, and I am even inclined to advocate the use of the ordinary words 'passes,' etc., in the sense of 'passes$_1$.' In short, I think that what is required is merely some additional primitive terms, and not that 'passes,' etc., should be understood in a different sense, even though I admit that there are other senses of 'passes' which are closer to standard usage. The trouble is that these senses are extraordinarily vague, whereas 'passes$_1$' is completely clear.

5. Consider, for example, the quite different way of using the basic tonal terms which amounts to approximately the following: y passes from x to z if and only if: (1) 'passes$_1$' holds, but *also* (2) this relation occurs on some level of a correct (or adequate) Schenkerisation of the piece. Let us use subscripts '2' for this usage. Now a certain complication is inevitable here unless we are willing to make the extremely dubious assumption that for any piece whatsoever, no matter how incoherent or 'atonal,' there exists one and only one correct Schenkerisation of it.

Namely, we will have to specify *which* Schenkerisation we are concerned with, at least to the extent of whether 'y passes$_2$ from x to z' and 'y passes$_2$ from u to w' are both true with respect to the split into further distinctions which we may indicate by a subscript letter following the number. Thus 'y passes$_{2,A}$ from x to z' means that y passes$_1$ from x to z on some level of the Schenkerisation A, and A is adequate.

(Moreover, a still more annoying complication arises if we are not willing to assume that correctness or adequacy of a Schenkerisation is an absolute term, but only that some Schenkerisations are more adequate than others. For even though there may be only finitely many

Schenkerisations (including even the most inadequate or preposterous ones) of a given piece, it still does not follow that there is a unique most adequate one or even a unique set of most adequate ones, unless the relation of being more-adequate-than has certain properties of ordering. In particular, it had better be asymmetrical and transitive, or at least not symmetrical and intransitive. This question may seem ludicrous, but since no one has given the slightest evidence one way or the other, or even made any serious attempt to define adequacy in any sense, we have to consider it.

What we *can* say is this: no matter what the structure of the relation more-adequate-than may be, we can define absolute adequacy in the following minimal sense: A Schenkerisation is *absolutely adequate* if and only if there is no other Schenkerisation of the same piece which is more adequate. This might turn out to be useless in that there might never be any absolutely adequate Schenkerisation of any piece, but this is the best we can do.)

6. Now it seems obvious that 'passes$_2$' is closer to ordinary usage of 'passes' than is 'passes$_1$.' But on the other hand, it seems plausible that if more-adequate-than could be precisely defined, 'passes$_{2\phi}$' would, for any ϕ, be translatable into some term of the "Subscript '1' language."

In fact, I think this is more than likely, it is practically certain. The following argument will attempt to show this.

(1) For a given piece, there *may* be infinitely many Schenkerisations. For example, if there is an operation of 'erasure' whereby a tone on some level is removed from the next, then evidently the same tone could be erased and put back in see-saw fashion n times for any n, and there would be at least one Schenkerisation for each n. But the same consequence follows from much less dubious operations. For example, if there is an operation of octave transfer, then one may transfer the same tone back and forth between the same two registers n times for any n. Moreover, if some way could be found for reducing repetitions to single operations (which is not easy since other operations might intervene, etc.), one could still transfer a tone up n octaves for any n, one at a time, and then back again. Suppose that this is forbidden on the ground that the audible pitch range must not be exceeded, or some other ground. Then plenty of other ways of circumventing such prohibitions still exist. For example, given any tone, we can merely re-attack it half-way through its duration, and this process can be applied again to the first attack, and so on. But then *by virtue of a suspension of some previous tone in the same line*, all of these repetitions of attack can be

wiped out. Thus anywhere that there is a suspension, we have infinitely many Schenkerisations according to how many times the absent portion of the resolving tone was subdivided. Perhaps, after all, some way of ruling out *all* such absurdities can be found. Certainly the problem is far from trivial. In the above case, for example, the reason why the subdivisions are forbidden seems to be that some *subsequent* operation is going to be applied. Here we may perhaps argue that this is not really so; what is incorrect is the suspension itself, on the ground that a suspension is forbidden to wipe out rhythmic distinctions. In other cases, it is not too clear that this argument will stand up.

At any rate, my point is not that there *are* infinitely many Schenkerisations of a given piece, but rather that we may so choose to construe the situation, and that there are serious problems involved in the opposite assumption.

(2) However, it also seems clear that except for finitely many of the Schenkerisations of a given piece, *the rest are all less adequate than some other*. And though we *cannot* give a general definition of more-adequate-than, for all these cases *we can immediately construct a more adequate one*. Now suppose that every Schenkerisation for which a more adequate one is immediately constructable is left out of account; then it seems clear that the remainder will have a finite number. Thus in particular there will merely be only finitely many Schenkerisations than which there is no more adequate one, at most. Indeed, this is a much *weaker* conclusion than that there are only finitely many for which no more adequate one is immediately constructible. This argument can be strengthened by noting that since every piece may be construed as having only finitely many events (except for infinite processes generated by some sort of repetition, which presumably could be Schenkerised by a correlated infinite process), in order for there to be infinitely many *absolutely* adequate Schenkerisations, some process would have to exist whereby from any given Schenkerisation, some *more* adequate one could be constructed; moreover, *there could be no upper bound to the number of operations* in a Schenkerisation for it to be less adequate than some other, even relative to the number of events in the piece; since the operations themselves are of course finitely numerous.

Therefore it seems to be hardly possible to doubt that there exist only finitely many absolutely adequate Schenkerisations of a given piece.

Incidentally, by a similar argument we could make it hardly possible to doubt that in general there exist only finitely many absolutely adequate *analyses* of any piece, and hence, that in principle it is possible to state a complete compendium of everything relevant to analysis of a piece, in the sense that anything anyone might say subsequently would be prevalent to an analysis less adequate than one already given. Whether it would be physically possible for a human to understand and remember such a compendium is another matter.

[intervening material]

7. We are now in a position to throw some light on just why Schenker's theory is so confused. To begin with, he confused the "Subscript-'1'" concepts with the "Subscript-'2'" concepts.

[intervening material]

By this of course I do not mean that he confused, e.g., 'passes$_1$' with 'passes$_2$'—this would have been too crude a mistake. But he did think that by adding further conditions and riders to "Subscript-'1'" terms, as we did in defining P_1, he could arrive at a general definition of 'passing$_2$.' And this still seems to be the general view of those who do Schenkerisations—for while they are always producing complicated and obscure reasons why 'passes' does or does not hold in some given case, they hardly ever consider the general question of what makes one Schenkerisation preferable to another, and even when they do there is certainly no hint of any belief that the meaning of 'passes' might depend on this question. But if, as seems obvious, the latter question in turn depends on that of what, in general, makes one analysis of any piece better than another, then there is clearly no reason to believe that 'more-adequate-Schenkerisation-than' is definable in terms of "Subscript-'1'" terms; and hence there is no reason to believe that "Subscript-'2'" terms are definable in terms of "Subscript-'1'" terms; and in particular, 'passes$_2$' is almost certainly not definable in terms of "Subscript-'1'" terms, no matter how complicated the conditions are made. *Thus the reason that no one has been able to clearly specify the conditions under which a tone is or is not a passing tone is not just that it is a very difficult problem, but that in the sense of 'conditions' and 'passing' in use, the problem is in principle insoluble.* If Schenker-style analysis is to be clarified, we must choose between (A) using only the "Subscript-'1'" language, and accepting the consequence that all such questions as whether a given tone is or is not a passing tone (except in the trivial sense of 'passes$_1$') must simply be shelved as irrelevant, and (B) attempting to explicate the general notion of better-analysis-than. Any other course is doomed to eternal confusion.

8. The distinction between "Subscript-'1'" and "Subscript-'2'" terms may be put to other uses. For example, the question of whether, if x is a neighbor to y, y can also be a neighbor to x, is of course a matter of how we intend to understand 'neighbor.' But specifically, if we understand it in the sense of 'neighbor$_1$,' it clearly can, and moreover, in one plausible sense of 'neighbor$_1$,' *invariably is*. On the other hand, if 'neighbor$_2$' is intended, I think our best course is simply to admit that in view of the present vagueness of the notion of better-analysis-than, we can hardly marshal enough evidence even to make one answer seem more plausible than the other. We know, of course, that this is assumed to be impossible by almost all Schenkerisers. But we fail to see any particular grounds for this belief.

VII.

N2: 68–71

This excerpt is one of Winham's most interesting discussions of the phenomenal nature of musical time as it applies to analysis.

The *primarily affected time-span* of a linearly subordinate element is the time from its beginning until the beginning of the next element in the series generated by the operation, or the main element in the case of a minimal motion.

This time-span thus varies according to what we consider the next element to be; on the other hand, what we consider the original main tone (or previous element in the series of a non-minimal motion) to be has no effect on the time-span, because this cannot begin before the element concerned is begun. In practice we must usually consider several different time-spans for the same element, because typically tonal music distributes the various plausible qualities of a main tone for a given element over several different subsequent tones.

In this sense the time-span of a complete progression has an *essential* main tone (the one that comes at the end and thus defines the time-span of the subordinate tone) and an *inessential* main tone (the one which comes at the beginning and does not affect the subordinate span).

In the case of the neighbor, the inessential main tone is also inessential in the sense that it need not occur at all; this is not true for the passing progression, because the initial main tone is essential to define the interval through which the tones pass (it is perhaps conceivable, nevertheless, that this tone might be omitted by an inferior operation; but I know of no clear case where this analysis seems plausible). In other words, a neighbor may be applied by replacement of the initial segment of the main element. Theoretically it might also replace the terminal segment; but in this case it would have an indefinitely extending time-span. Hence this is most plausible at the end of a piece.

A justification for this asymmetrical view of the definition of time-spans might be found in the mere fact of the attack of a tone coming at its beginning. I.e., if we consider time-spans as defined only by attacks, then the time-span of a progression runs from the attack of the first main element to the attack of the final one, and the subordinate element in a minimal progression is then more closely associated with the final main element in that its time-span occupies the final segment of the progression.

This argument has problems in particular cases, however (e.g., a succession of staccatos).

Instead, we should appeal to the concept of effective context. The final main tone (or 'resolving tone') includes the subordinate tone in its effective context, while the original main tone does not. Or better: the (subordinate tone + final main tone) has the same effective context as the main tone by itself; by one of our basic assumptions, this is a similarity—indeed the analogy with the relation of derivative to root is obvious (the similarity of part to whole). On the contrary, however, the (original main tone + subordinate tone) has the same effective context not as the main tone but as the subordinate one. For this reason it may be argued that in every succession of two events there is a ground for regarding the second as the 'main' one, i.e., that it has a similarity to the sum.

But this is probably pushing the concept too far. It seems to conflict with another plausible idea, viz. that the earlier event is more important because it belongs to a more effective context.

The concept of definition of time-spans by the beginnings of events is all right in itself, but our explanation of this is faulty.

What is needed is a definition of 'hanging' which makes use of the notion of effective context, with the result that a tone is not hanging before it occurs.

An event x may be said to be effective at the time of an event y if and only if x belongs to the effective context of y.

An event x may be said to be closed off from y if it is subordinate to another event z which is between x and y in time.

An event x is hanging at the time of an event y if it belongs to the effective context of y and is not closed off from y, although there is a superior stage at which it *is* closed off from y. (If the latter is not the case, it is said to be 'retained' rather than hanging.) The difference between 'retained' and 'hanging' is thus relative to a set of sketches.

The idea that being later makes a tone ipso facto more important is based on the idea that the later tone belongs to all the same effective contexts as itself plus the earlier one(s), and is thus equivalent to this sum in the sense that they are effective at all the same times. But this is true for the earlier tone by itself too except for the short time up to the end of itself, so this difference is very small.

It is probably incorrect to think of this as a similarity in the same sense as other qualitative similarities. It seems preferable to relate it to our original idea that the composition consists of the set of its effective contexts.

A possible alternative is to consider the effectiveness of all earlier events at a given time as itself a basic assumption. (This might make it possible to preserve the idea that there is just *one* total pattern.)

(The fallacy in our earlier deduction may be this: events that end at the same time are effective as wholes at all the same time; but an event which has not yet ended ought to be considered partly effective once it has begun, if we are going to consider nonminimal events at all.)

It could be argued that if we are going to consider the piece as a set of effective contexts, then each such context ought to be viewed as having its last events *nearest* in time. This relation would be similar to emphasis. This is very likely correct; but there still may be a simpler method which is not incorrect.

In answer to this argument, in any case, it could be argued that there is a fundamental distinction between presence and absence only; that temporal remoteness, beyond this, is not fundamental. And since an effective context, i.e., a time, is identified by its last or present events, there is no need to make any further distinction.

VIII.

*26d

This text gives Winham's most elaborate attempt to precisely model the sort of relations uncovered in analysis. The first section is relatively straightforward. The second section, where he expands the opening material as a theory of prolongation, I find more puzzling. The various rules he gives for the elaboration of locales, however, seem to work out in strict counterpoint. The numbering in this excerpt is confusing.

01. Each tone has various functions, which are divided (1) into *Necessary* and *Unnecessary* (always capitalized to avoid confusion with the simple root-meanings, though these are related), and (2) into a hierarchy of Higher and Lower functions, which, however, is not simply a series but a more complicated structure, as will be seen. This hierarchy applies only to the Necessary functions in the first instance; a similar hierarchy could be described for the others, but this will not be done here and would be of less significance.

02. Each function determines a group of tones, in relation to which the function exists. Such a group will be termed a *locale*. Each locale is a locale-of-function of each of its constituent tones.

The nature of a locale determines relations of *Superiority* or *Inferiority* among its constituent tones, thus: *A tone x is inferior to another y if there exists a locale in which the relation of x to y is a Necessary function of y but not of x.*

It is evident that of a given pair of tones, neither need be superior, as there may be no locale which is a locale of function of both. Moreover there may exist two different locales including both x and y, such that x is both superior and inferior to y. *However, in all such cases one of these locales is a sub-group of the other, and the subgroup is an incomplete locale in the sense defined below.* Thus with this rare but important exception, superiority of x to y excludes the reverse relation.

03. All *incomplete* locales are such that they would remain (correct) locales if other tones were added; but this cannot be used as a definition because there exist cases of extendible complete locales. The following definition is correct: a locale is incomplete if one of its *temporally outer* tones is inferior to another of its tones. Thus a complete locale is one in which the temporally outer tones have no superiors in the locale. The relations of inferiority referred to must be determined by the locale itself, however. Thus, strictly: a locale is incomplete if it contains a temporally outer tone x, inferior to another tone y of the locale *by virtue of the relation constituting the locale.* It does not effect the issue if there exists some other locale in which x is inferior to y. Note: The locales include all of Schenker's 'Zug's' but include other groups also; moreover, when counting a 'zug' as a locale, one must take care to exclude all tones which are irrelevant to the zug's being such. If this is not clear, the fault lies with the vagueness of 'zug' and not with 'locale' which is a precise term, as will be seen.

The concept of 'level' is rejected here because it is based on two conceptual confusions: 1. The idea that the superiority relation constitutes a series; 2. The idea that it is necessary or even possible to order the locales (or zugs) themselves as to Higher and Lower (or more-or-less foreground or background), rather than the functions of their constituent tones.

One may still speak of levels-of-function of the single tone (if one remembers that not all of these levels are nicely arranged in series); but obviously this does not justify the practice of making a series of reductions of the whole piece and calling each successive one a higher level, a practice which is easily demonstrated to be arbitrary and misleading.

04(a). In certain cases one finds two functions of a tone, of which evidently at least one is Necessary, but not both. The decision as to which is the Necessary one is then made as follows: the types of locales are ordered as to simplicity-of-technique (though this order, again, is not a simple series); the simpler locale is then taken as the one determined by the Necessary function.

(E.g., if a tone is both a lower neighbor to the third degree and also a passing tone in a 3–2–1, the 3 being the same one, the latter is taken as its Necessary function, on the grounds that the former demonstrates a more advanced technique in that it contradicts the tendency of the tone 2. The other function is not thereby denied, but counts as Unnecessary).

04(b). More rarely, this type of 'choice' may be between two functions which are mutually exclusive in that they offend the rule that x cannot be both superior and inferior to y in different locales (unless one is a subgroup of the other). In this case too the decision is based on which function demonstrates the simpler technique; and in this case the other one must be held not to exist at all. (The reason for this rule will emerge when we discuss examples.)

11. We now define the properties of a (correct) locale. First, the locales must be divided into two classes, those that are such only by virtue of *pitch-class relationships* (i.e., which contain octave transferences and resolutions to 'implied' tones, etc.), and those in which the correctness of the locale is demonstrable without reference to such relationships. We concentrate first on the latter, which are again divided into Fundamental and Non-fundamental locales.

A Fundamental locale is (1) in strict counterpoint; (2) contains bass tones which outline the triad supporting the temporally outer tone; (3) does not contain any incomplete locales except those which are subgroups of complete ones.

E.g., a I–IV–V–I progression cannot be a Fundamental locale, because the bass does not outline the I triad. V–I is not fundamental because it is incomplete: the temporally outer tones of the V chord are inferior to the following ones. To show this from our definition of inferiority: (1) Given two such chords, only V–I interprets them so that the bass outlines I. (2) On that basis, the upper tones of the V chord are not Necessary from the point of view of their resolutions, as a I chord by itself is a correct locale. (3) But on the contrary, the resolving tones are Necessary, given the interpretation of the upper tones on the first chord as supported by V. (4) Hence the latter are inferior. (5) Hence the locale is incomplete, as it contains temporally outer inferior tones.

A Non-fundamental locale is either (1) a Fundamental locale but with the initial tonic missing, (2) a Fundamental locale plus other tones which, however, *do not result in the existence of smaller fundamental locales.* In the latter case each such added tone must obey the following rules:

1. It must be followed directly by a tone a step away from it, or indirectly provided the resolving tone is not inferior to any intervening tone.

2. The step involved must belong to the scale whose tonic is the chord supporting the resolving tone, or to a scale whose tonic is one of the chords supporting tones to which the resolving tone is inferior by virtue of the Fundamental locale.*

   *[Or the same thing a further stage removed, and so on; i.e.: the tone belongs to a scale whose tonic is superior in the locale to the tones which are superior to the resolving tone, etc. (I know of no such complicated case, but see no reason why it should not exist.)]

   E.g., I–IV–V–I qualifies because the IV–V step in the bass belongs to the scale of I. I–#IV–V–I is also correct, and does not result in a smaller locale (VII–I of V) because the latter (containing the diminished triad) is not in strict counterpoint. And I–(V of V)–V–I still counts as a locale, because the smaller locale it contains (V–I of V) is not Fundamental (because of its incompleteness).

   All of these examples of course presuppose stepwise voice-leading in the upper parts. If this does not hold, they may still be locales, but then they are of the class requiring the concept of pitch-class step-connections.

3. Additional restrictions on the diatonic-scale to which the tones added to the Fundamental locale may belong are not necessary, because cases which would violate these will always create smaller Fundamental locales. However, it is necessary to add further restrictions having to do with the tendencies of these tones when they do belong to an appropriate diatonic scale. Specifically, I believe that the following is the correct formulation: If a tone x is to be counted as resolving to a tone z (to fulfill the above rules), and there exists an intervening tone y (which we have already said,

must not be superior to z), then if x is a step away from z and is not superior to z, *its tendency must be in the other direction.*

This is complicated so it had better be illustrated by a diagram. The tone x is to be counted as resolving to z despite its also being countable as resolving to the intervening y.

$$x \rightarrow y \Rightarrow z$$

This is possible in the first place only if y is not superior to z. But in addition, the tendency of x must be in the direction of z, not of y.

The idea is that otherwise the tone y completely resolves the instability of x, so that in the step-connection x–z cannot have this function. Note: These rules have the effect that of two tones in a locale which are a step apart and temporally adjacent, one must be superior to the other by virtue of the locale. And the same is true of temporally adjacent tones forming a harmonic interval (other than the octave or unison) if the locale is a Fundamental one. But a Non-fundamental locale need not of itself determine any such relation.

6. [sic] Connection and inclusion of locales.

The basic rule, without which all hell would break loose, has already been given: that no two locales (except if one is included in the other) may result in reversing a superiority relation between the two tones. Secondly, we can limit further the cases in which this arises with one locale including another: the two tones involved are invariably a step apart. Let them be x and y. Now one of them (say y) is always inferior and related by step to a third tone z, from which x is a third away. In fact y is a passing tone from x to z, but also x is a neighbor to y. Thus we see why this simple case arises: because of the existence of two types of inferiority—(1) of the subsidiary tone to its origin and resolution, (2) of the tone forming a harmonic interval with another tone, the triad concerned being such that the former is the subordinate tone (i.e., III versus V, or III versus I). As long as only one of these types is involved, superiority can be kept unidirectional. But it would be impossible to prevent this special case from arising except by excluding neighbor-tones from being themselves elaborated with unprepared neighbors in the same direction (since this technique automatically results in a harmonic interval with the middle tone as a passing tone).

The obligation to keep the superiority relations uni-directional furnishes the controlling criterion for the elaboration of a local decoration of its members with further locales of which they are the most superior tones. (This could be more simply done by insisting that each locale be fundamental, of course. This would result in a radically more elementary system.)

7. Order of simplicity of]techniques.

This serves not only the function of deciding certain issues, as already mentioned, but also is an interesting aspect of this description in itself. (E.g., one may show that in a certain piece the techniques introduced gradually become more advanced, etc.). The order is as follows: 1. Among the techniques allowed in strict composition, the order is the usual one (first note against note, then 2 notes, etc.). 2. The above only result in fundamental locales. The next two techniques are respectively—

(1) leaving off the origin (unprepared subsidiary tones and harmonies).
(2) Insertions such as covert fundamental locales into non-fundamental ones. These are then ordered according to how many further functions they give to any tone, at most (the fewer, the simpler of course).

3. octave techniques, ordered as follows:

(1) simple doubling of a complete voice
(2a) doubling incomplete voices, but in such a way that top and bass are unaffected.
(2b) doubling such as to create different top and bottom lines. Here it becomes necessary to add rules (see below).
(3a) motion by octave + (or −) step instead of direct step.
(3b) the same, with top or bottom affected. (Note: there is no order as between (2b) and (3a). This is an example of this not being a simple series.)
(4) resolution to 'implied' tones: e.g., a V7 is followed by a I represented simply by an octave. The resolving third is not present at all; nevertheless this technique exists. The order, as between the series (2) and (3), is again not a very definite matter, as two different kinds of things are concerned, which can hardly be quantitatively compared.

IX.

*30ab

This text develops the notion of the deviant hierarchy. "A.K." is Arthur Komar. "J.R." is (I believe) Jim Randall. The concluding section, wherein Winham concludes that hierarchy is best taken as giving parameters of surface tones, is key to his conception of the place and function of analysis.

> 1. The background-foreground distinction is essentially one of size: but there are two complicatory factors: (1) While a larger & a smaller passage may have 'the same' overall pattern, the larger one has it by virtue of more complicated considerations. E.g. in order to show that the overall pattern of a movement is I–V–I, it is necessary to show that all events within a larger span are in some sense reducible to one chord V, etc.; in the foreground this may be so in a very simple sense. (2) A reduction does not treat every time-span, but only a hierarchy of time-spans related by what essentially amounts to *inclusion*. However, other time-spans may have some of the same characteristics as one belonging to the hierarchy.

E.g. in Beethoven's G-major sonata [Op.49, #2], m.2 belongs to the hierarchy, & so does its second half, within which there is an accented-nb. relation. M.1.5–2.5 [Ed.: the midpoint of the second measure to the midpoint of the third measure] is a non-hierarchic time-span; but the second half of m.2 is hierarchically subordinate to this span, and within this half measure, so considered, there is a passing-tone relation of G to F♯. Thus the 'sense' of the second half of m.2 depends on whether it is considered as such or as the first half of m.1.5–2.5.

Moreover the decision that this is a non-hierarchic time-span does not follow from its metric sense alone, because it might result from the half-measure 'anticipation' applied to m.3 as a unit (i.e., because the hierarchic time-spans are *not* generated strictly by inclusion *only*). In a sense this is a re-simplifying point; i.e., most non-hierarchic time-spans are eventually subordinate to hierarchic ones.

Furthermore, the non-hierarchic status of m.1.5–2.5 may be said to *consist* in its overlapping of a time-span (m.3) which is assumed in the derivation which results in its being considered at all; except that since the anticipation may be considered to be applied only to the *first half* of m.3, this may have to be weakened to read: to *consist* in its including a time-span whose initial point stands higher in the hierarchy than its own initial point. This is the same as A.K.'s notion of a 'syncopated time-span' except that it requires that the syncopation be evident from the derivation (i.e., some span at the beginning of m.3 must actually be invoked in order to make m.1.5–2.5 non-hierarchic; this is so here, of course).

2. There are several obscurities remaining.

If there is no limit on the development of such 'deviant hierarchies,' one may wonder why it is usual in reductions not to even mention them; or if they *are* limited, why is this so?

Secondly, presumably in some cases 'hierarchic' spans may be considered deviant from the 'deviant' ones, and hence the question arises whether the difference is only a matter of degree; and again: if so, why should the best supported ones belong to a full hierarchy? But the answer to this is of course that they *don't*. Often a deviant span is better supported than an overlapping hierarchic one. One has to distinguish between spans which have well-developed subordinate hierarchies and spans which belong to a well-developed hierarchy in which they themselves are subordinate. We consider a span 'hierarchic' only if it belongs to a hierarchy developed all the way from largest to smallest spans. That there *is* any such hierarchy is the condition of the work being 'tonal.'

This leads to the answers to the first questions above. Deviant hierarchies are limited so that they shall not obscure the main one; and to the extent that they *do* occur, they *should* be mentioned.

3. The Beethoven example leads to other interesting considerations. Note that the second half of m.2 alone has a sense which fits with its hierarchic sense; i.e., to reduce it to simply ♩G/G does not involve invoking pitches outside the time-span. On the other hand, the sense of

the G's as passing tones does not appear until the first attack of the next measure is also taken into account. Thus the reduction to ♩ G/G can be considered a simple 'property' of the span, whereas the reduction to ♩ A/F♯ is 'relational.'

As against this it could be argued that the first attack of m.3 is necessary to *define* the span concerned by ending it; from this point of view the situation seems exactly reversed! For while the reduction to ♩ A/F♯—F♯/A is now clearly a 'property' of the span, the reduction to ♩ G/G—A/F♯ does not make sense at all; i.e., it is necessary to at least consider only the portion of the span excluding its final point in order to make the reduction to ♩ G/G a property of something. Rather than this it seems preferable to consider it a property of the ♩ span from ♩ A/F♯ to G/G. As a 'property' of the ♩ span it is then only 'relational' to some smaller span within this. I.e., it seems preferable to consider spans to *always* contain their final points if they *ever* do so.

In this case, however, the implication is that subdivision into quarters is prior to introduction of the nb. on the first quarter.

In support of the view that spans do not include their final points, it could be argued that the relevance of the final point (in determining that something is 'passing') is not especially different from that of some earlier point outside the time-span (which may determine that something is 'suspended,' or even more analogously: that something is an 'accented passing tone'). This is surely true, in that for example the goal of a passing tone may itself be delayed by suspension.

3. [sic.] Another question is why, if these hierarchies are essentially defined just by inclusion of time-spans, we should regard them as constructions from the highest member.

For example, we describe a 3–2–1 motion by considering the 2 as substituted for a continuing 3; or: we describe this whole span as containing an E–C arpeggiation.

The latter description is 'correct' in that while the E is not *actually* continued, what happens instead is derivable from it by the passing tone operation (we prefer to consider this a substitution rather than the filling of a rest, because we regard the subdivision of the E–C timespan as defined *by* the D & not 'already' defined in any case).

So far we are just saying that the actual passage has something in common with just E–C, viz. its outer attack points, etc. But now suppose the E is inflected by an F appoggiatura. This does not preserve the temporal or registral outerness of E *in the time-span under consideration*; it does of course preserve them if we alter the time-span under consideration to exclude the F, by front-end truncation or compression. But this operation does not preserve the rhythmic characteristics of the original (e.g., that D was at the midpoint of E–C or after it, so that E was at least as long as D). Thus we have a dilemma: if these characteristics are essential in what is preserved in the passing operation, then they should not be removed by some other operation, & therefore we must consider what is preserved in the *same* time-span; but if the temporal & spatial outerness of the E is essential, then we must *reduce* the time-span to exclude F.

The answer seems to be that both are essential, but that an operation need not preserve them both in the same entity; i.e., it may preserve one in one entity and transfer the other to some other entity instead. Thus the sequence of operations used here yields the outline of the original in a reduced time-span & the rhythm of the original in the same time-span. The whole span still has attacks at the same points; the reduced span has the tone the whole had before. It is essential here, however, that the reduction is to a time-span closely related to the original one (here it is included in it). Moreover, this still does not adequately describe the situation; for clearly the reduction of the original time-span must in some sense preserve the E's influence from the beginning of the original time-span.

If there is independent good reason to think of the F as a substitute for E, this in itself is sufficient, of course. On the other hand, the necessity of such a 'thought' in order to explain the D as a weak passing tone is itself some reason for it. Moreover, it must be admitted that we can think of the F in this way *without* knowing any 'reason' at all. E.g.., if there is a C under F–E, we can of course point to the increasing consonance as F moves to E, etc.; or if another E precedes the F, we can point to the temporal enclosure of the F by E's. But the idea that F substitutes for E here is not exhaustible by any conjunction or alternation of such conditions. It depends ultimately only on the possibility of a 'good analysis,' containing it, for the whole piece.

This seems to make it more urgent to formulate this thought as one 'about' the foreground as it stands; i.e., to say the F *is* a nb. to E & *is* inferior to it. Hence, the D *is* a weak passer in the sense that though its original pitch does not occur on a stronger beat, what does occur there *is* 'inferior to' or 'a nb. to' a tone of that pitch.

A difficulty here is that it is usual to explain such statements in terms of derivation, whereas our point here is that such explanations themselves require explanation in terms of characterization of the foreground. This is so because in thinking of the F as a nb. we do not actually mean to say it *was* derived by substituting for E, nor merely that it could have been; nor even that such a derivation could be part of a consistent process of such derivations (for there might be other consistent compositional processes to arrive at this result besides those which happen to proceed from the background to the foreground). Rather, we are thinking that the actual passage (F–E) has, in this context or relative to this context, some property which E alone would also have. This property would seem to be something like "coherence with the rest of the piece in so far as only time-spans of a certain size or larger are considered." This coherence is presumably more obvious in the case of E alone, so that we reduce F–E to E alone in order to *reveal* it; also no doubt it is not as good (at least in some respects) with the F—i.e., we still have to consider the smaller spans in order to explain the F fully; up to this point we have merely shown that it does not prevent them from cohering with one another.

In this much, we are in essential agreement with J.R., i.e., we agree that the statements of reductive analysis are statements about the foreground, not about how it was or could have been constructed. It follows, as he says, that the 'notes' of higher levels are actually parameters of the foreground notes, however indirectly (it *does not* follow that they have no 'durations;' they can just as well have these as 'pitches,' obviously). However, since the whole piece has to be considered, in principle, to determine any of these parameters, they are really *all* 'global' in one sense.

We have seen that there is some difficulty in deciding just what they are parameters *of*, too; but no doubt this problem is soluble, in that the first-level parameters must be 'of' certain particular foreground elements, *not* including all those which have to be considered to decide them.

X.

*16

This passage uses an extended and sensitive reading of the opening of the second movement of Beethoven's Op. 111 as a means of holding together the discussion of a wide range of ideas relating to analysis.

The pattern in the large would seem to be (I–V–I)–V; no unusual features are presented in the first beats, which define the harmonics expected from the melodic upbeats. From this point of view beats 2 and 3 of m.1 represent anticipations of m.2. M.3 has no anticipation; but the harmony of m.4 is the same anyway because of the 6/4 suspen-

ARIETTA.

Adagio molto semplice e cantabile.

sion. In m.2 we have an ambiguity in that I occurs on beat 2, and this could represent anticipation as in m.1; but it could also pass to beat 3, through intervals also defined in m.1.

In any event it is also possible to regard the large pattern as V–I–I–V; the upbeats are then associated with suspension (of 'all' voices). In this case the C in m.2's bass must be superior to the D following, because the other possibility yields 2 measures of V consecutively, which can be ruled out in view of the melodic pattern.

This way of looking at the passage seems wrong *because only one of the interpretations of the C–D in the bass of m.3 fits with it.*

In any case the *other* interpretation is preferable because the passing of the alto F to G fits better with the D–E motion of the upper voice than would a nb.-motion back to F. If anticipation in m.2 were the main point, it should have been G/E which occurred at beat 2, corresponding to F/D in m.1; also perhaps the melody should have contained an anticipation of E.

In other words, the interpretation of m.2 with E as a passer is preferable because it allows the following F to be part of a general derivation of the alto in parallel sixths with the melody throughout the four measures. Given this, the interpolation of a passing I chord is comprehensible; it still substitutes for the previous first inversion V just as F/D in m.1 substituted for I, even though by a 'different' technique. But if the techniques are regarded as 'the same' (anticipation), the function of the F in m.2 is obscured, since it is not derived with the melodic D as a passer from the original E.

In terms of ordered construction from the background this is all clear; the F must be derived before the E to give it the right sense, whereas the E has much the same sense in any case. Yet we know from other examples that the occurrence of an E displacing F and superior to it does not remove all possible connection to a later F; indeed in this case we could say that anticipating E first allows the large E–F–G motion to be decorated by a small one. The preference for deriving F before E here seems based essentially on the idea of F's greater 'necessity.' I.e., given E we must have another F (else there will be no F–G connection to speak of); but given F the E is not particularly necessary, since the anticipation essentially belongs to the first two units (c.f. the melody) and not the 3rd. In other words it seems to be based on the idea that the construction from background to foreground is the logical explanatory order, which has already been rejected in that correction of defects in the middleground is considered a possible motivation for foreground elaboration.

Another approach starts by recognizing that there is a conflict here; the factors which support one interpretation are against the other at least in that they fail to support it. Thus the fact that C is itself registrally enclosed by B and D weakens the outline C–E; but conversely the enclosure of D weakens the outline E–D. The overall outline B–E is harmonically irrelevant. The B–D outline is predefined in m.1, but the C–E outline is confirmed in m.3. (These are of course not equivalent factors; the relevance of m.1 is much greater because of its precedence.) The C–E outline has the advantage of being tonic; the B–D has the advantage of its metrical sense (defined by *length* in the melody, as well as by the metrical clarity of m.3).

Whether these factors are in balance or not, they continue to exist.

Now we must ask—just what is it that they support? The answer presumably is that they support certain larger patterns. Those factors supporting B/D support the parallel-sixth motion of the upper voices; those supporting C/E support the continuance of the 'anticipation' rhythms (i.e., the conflict of weights of beats 1 and 2, and also the change of harmony in the melody at beat 3). The support for the former is becoming stronger (the sixths become literal shortly), whereas the latter is gradually weakened (beat 1 becomes definitive for the measure in the bass at m.4). On this ground the enclosure of G is perhaps 'perceptually stronger' in somewhat the same way that a tone which is getting louder is 'stronger' than one which is getting softer (at the moment where they are in some sense equal).

'Reduction' in this case is bound to remove the anticipation-pattern before it removes the parallel sixths (although the latter may recede into 'latency'); thus the B/D also has the advantage of relevance to the more background patterning factor.

Indeed the foreground rhythm here can be explained as basically 'having' the function of removing octave and fifth parallels; in the course of this they remove some of the sixth parallels as well, but these are allowed to survive in the literal foreground towards the end of the passage, where no octave and fifth parallels are 'threatened.' However, (Schenker to the contrary) we know that not all rhythmic factors will be explainable in this way.

Still, it is worth noting that only certain particular kinds of 'defects' are removed by foreground elaboration; perhaps these all fall into the category of 'excessive simplicity' in some sense, as with parallels or block-chordal motions (which therefore do not sufficiently define inner-voice motions or differentiate lengths of superior and inferior spans).

Thus if it is a defect that F in m.2 moves to E in m.3 (because then it cannot be strongly connected to G), this defect might be held irremediable by foreground elaboration. In other words, this defect is correctable because it results in a possible interpretation in a different order of priority. In this case, the F→E defect is correctable by insertion of another F only because then the first E can be regarded as passing to F. (This may have a meaning of the following sort: if the alto D's at mm.2 and 3 are replaced by D's, the large F–G connection is destroyed because it is no longer reasonable to regard the E in m.3 as passing.)

This brings up another point: although we claim that background → foreground construction is not the only plausible method, it does not follow that *any* order is plausible.

Indeed, perhaps the only plausible orders are those which are *consistent with* background–foreground construction; in the sense that we may elaborate a middle V before the surrounding I's, for example, but we may not *add* the surrounding I's to an already given V. But then in cases of ambiguity we will have to say that two orders have some plausibility and some implausibility; and the coherence of the result will depend on the possibility of both. But since this coherence is itself a matter of degree, we will have to conclude that all orders having any degree of plausibility (insofar as they in any degree undermine the plausibility of other orders, which is to say: roughly always) must be considered.

What this goes to show is that the mere derivation of all the tones according to tonal operations does not in itself have even the minimal virtue of providing one explanation for every tone. This is so only if the derivations form a coherent process. Even if they do, moreover, a 'bad' explanation may be the result, in the sense that another explanation may have the same virtues only more so.

Since belonging to the reductive hierarchy is not in itself any virtue, it follows that distinguishing local reductions by this means is futile. However, they may still be distinguished by belonging to hierarchies characterized by coherent process. But in the 'really ambiguous' cases this still does not suffice; both local reductions belong to coherent extensions of a background. Both belong to processes extending over the whole four-measure unit, in Op.111.

In contrast, in the G-major sonata [Op.49, II] the anticipation of F♯/A is not part of any such process, whereas the accented nb. F♯ fits with the corresponding D–C in m.4 and also with the accented half-note V in m.3, etc.

Allegro, ma non troppo.

‖ I–V- ‖ -I–V- ‖ -I : The V's here may be equally strong; in this case we consider each to subdivide its own half into quarters. Or it may be that the second V is much stronger; in this case we consider it to arise through a ♩. ♩ subdivision. But thirdly, it may be that the second V is somewhat stronger, but not greatly so; in this case we may consider both subdivisions relevant. For example at the beginning of the *Pathetique* slow movement, the fourth ♩ involves the outer parts in motion and is also more consonant than the second ♩ because D♭ does not appear until the 8th ♪. More critically still, it reconnects with the bass A♭, which was not displaced in register at the 2nd ♩. Nevertheless it represents a 'parallelism' with the 2nd ♩ and may be considered a means of returning to a root-position I from the first-inversion I.

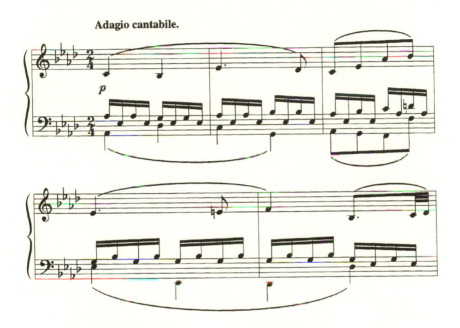

Adagio cantabile.

This represents a type of ambiguity which we do not worry much about because the 3rd ♩ is regarded as inferior to the 1st in any case. We consider the matter this way: the 2nd ♩ is inferior to the 1st & 3rd. The 4th is inferior to the 1st. The 3rd and 4th, however, are not necessarily ordered; hence also the 2nd and 4th are not necessarily ordered. But since even if the 4th is inferior to the 3rd it does not follow that it is inferior to the 2nd, whereas if the 4th is superior to the 3rd it must also be superior to the 2nd, the 4th has greater weight than the 2nd in this sense. In other words, this is not a real conflict; it simply reflects the ordering properties of a hierarchy as opposed to a series.

In Op.111, m.2, the case is different. Since beats 2 & 3 are related by displacements, it is assumed that one must be directly inferior to the other.

To put it another way: in the *Pathetique* the constructive order affects only the question of whether the fourth is to be regarded as passing from the 3rd or the 1st; but since these are 'the same,' it may be argued that it necessarily passes from both. In Op.111, however, beat 2 has a different 'sense' depending on whether it is superior or inferior to beat 3, since beat 3 is 'different' from the next measure, and similarly, beat 3 has a different sense depending on the same question, since beat 2 is 'different' from beat 1.

It could be argued that beat 3's sense is not really different, in that it still passes from E to G in any case. But this certainly does not hold for beat 2. On the other hand, beat 2's sense is in one way the same in any case, i.e., it is a substitute for V; but in this sense beat 3's meaning is different in the two cases; it either substitutes for the background I, or for a I which is itself a substitute for V (which is again a substitute for I).

The truth is surely that there *is* a difference here; that this measure has a 'real' ambiguity in the sense that m.1 of the *Pathetique* does not.

Still, this may perhaps merely indicate that even a hierarchy is not the right structure, just as the other (more trivial) type of ambiguity indicated that a series was not.

The modification suggested would be that either of beats 2 and 3 here could be considered superior; i.e., that the relation concerned is not strictly asymmetrical. This relation of mutual dependence is different from the mutual *in*dependence noted in other cases.

However, it seems to be the same as the relation between ♩s 3 and 4 in m.2 of the G-major sonata. The difference seems to lie only in the 'irrelevance' of one interpretation in that case (plus the somewhat greater complexity involved in the irrelevant interpretation in itself, but this is not great enough to be a major factor).

It may be noted that according to these assumptions the 4th element in a || I–V- | -I–V- || -I pattern, where it is 'equal' to the 2nd (e.g., where the two halves are simply identical), is therefore necessarily weightier than the 2nd in a certain sense—viz. that it passes only to the 3rd. Indeed this remains true even if the 2nd beat has *much* stronger support than the 4th—so long as it remains weaker than the 3rd; and it remains true in the same sense in the case of rhythms such as ♩ ♩ ♩ ... ♪, and even if the top voice here is, say, E–D–C–B- | -C. This presumes of course that something defines the measure (i.e., that the 1st beat is still stronger than the 3rd). This need not cause any alarm; for the 2nd beat is now stronger in another sense, viz. it is longer.

The usual reductive analysis is based on the assumption that these different kinds of emphasis can in some sense be added together to form a general quantity of 'structural weight' or 'support.' This seems unavoidable; but we can still profit from distinguishing certain situations where it is not as fruitful as in others.

A typical configuration is the | I– (V–X–V–) | I, where the X may be a weak I (e.g., over a V bass), or some other harmony such a VI. The characteristic feature is the strength of beat 2 compared to both beats 3 and 4; with respect to the comparison with beat 4, however, this may consist in no more than its partaking of the top-line continuity (e.g., if the notes are E–D–C–B–C), or even less: it may be just that given the inferiority of beat 3, beat 2 is superior to beat 4 by being the earlier element of a repetition.

The interesting point here is that if no rhythmic shifting is assumed we have the ♩ ♩. rhythm. There is a choice of various analyses which assume one prior attack of the V: 1. Simply [♩ ♩.] 2. [♩♩] with anticipation, thus: [♩♩♩] 3. [♩♩], the ♩ then being divided [♩♩] (i.e., anticipation of the form [♩—anticipated ♩—♩]).

It also may be possible, however, to consider two attacks of V to be introduced together (as with the passers in the interval of a fourth). In this case there is no particular virtue in assuming a background of ♩♩♩ because that would easily reduce to ♩♩. Similarly a background of ♩♩♩ would easily reduce to the same thing. So the point of this idea operates only if we consider the ♩♩♩ rhythm to be derivable directly from a whole note. (Call this 4.)

And the point is that this derivation uses the real attack of V as an excuse for its length; i.e., there is at least no direct ♩ length for this harmony as in 1. above.

It may be objected that the same idea is better carried out by (2), since here both attacks of V can be considered introduced together, by a similar process of great simplicity. This is true, but there remains something unsatisfactory about regarding the background beat for V as the one place where it does *not* occur in the foreground, when it *does* occur in *two* places other than that.

Another objection is that if the fact that the 2nd V is a repetition is to be ignored, we might equally ignore the fact that beat 3 is inferior in another sense. In other words, we might equally consider the rhythmic operation here to simply consist of dividing the ○ into four equal ♩s. This, however, does not have to mean going straight to the *harmonic* foreground. Rather, we can consider deriving from a ○ span a series of four ♩s in which the last 3 ♩s are all V. The advantage of this (5.) over (4.) is that first of all it is a simpler operation, and secondly the discrimination in favor of the 2nd beat over the 3rd does not enter until the next stage.

But it may well be objected that if this *were* the foreground we would have no objection to reducing it to ♩♩ after all; so that if the foreground should be reduced to this, we might as well adopt (2). In other words, there is no real point in going straight from 𝅝 to ♩♩♩♩ *unless we consider this to involve going straight to the foreground harmonies too.*

The idea involved here is that I–V–X–V makes a kind of sense as a subdivision of 𝅝 I which I–V–V–V does not; i.e., the occurrence of something *different from V* at beat 3, *even though inferior to V*, still functions to justify the rhythm of the I–V relation itself.

This might be explained by the possibility of a subsidiary interpretation in which the X is superior to the first V; for it does seem to be true that mere difference from V is not enough to suggest any nonanticipatory reduction—what is required in addition is that the X have some relation to the I, such as being diatonically consistent with it.

For example in Beethoven's Lydian chorale [Quartet Op.132] the F–E–D–E–F pattern might be rhythmically justified by the possibility of considering the first E a passing tone to D, even though this is not the 'main' interpretation. If, on the other hand, the D were supported by a "raised-IV" chord instead of the VI, we might prefer the anticipatory solution—precisely because B-natural refers to C and thus to some extent has the same affect as of repetition of the C chord.

It seems to follow, however, that to the extent that we are willing to accept this VI chord as a nb. chord, we should also be willing to accept interpretation (2) (at least in the form where ♩♩ becomes ♩♩♩♩; i.e., there is no need to consider the ♩♩ rhythm, since beat 4 can be derived together with beat 2).

The conclusion then would be that hierarchy does not have to have a rhythmic derivation which is sensible in itself; that instead it may be only by virtue of deviant hierarchies which are rhythmically simpler that the hierarchic rhythms are sensible. E.g. it may be appropriate to anticipate a harmony precisely *because* it will then also function as a rhythmically normal passing tone to something derived from it.

An entirely different approach is the idea that the ♩♩♩♩ rhythm here arises from bifurcation of the measure, the 4th ♩ being a reduplication of the 2nd. Thus the derivation is simply from ♩♩. But since the 'missing' beat here then corresponds to the final I, this just leads back to the same approach, essentially.

The minimal elements of the structure might be considered all single tones, regardless of the metric position of their beginnings and ends. Elements may have parts which are also relevant in some sense; but they need never be considered directly as elements of the reductive system. For example, we need not ask by what operation the suspended part of a tone is derived; we can consider the total tied tone as derived by some operation. When a suspension is attacked, this may be considered an extra operation of subdivision; but since the subdivision will not necessarily obey the usual rules of non-syncopation in this case, it may be preferable to consider it a transfer of the attack-feature of the prior displacement to the suspension. In other words, it would be preferably introduced together with the delay of the displacement. In any case the main point is that the case of non-attached suspensions can be handled without assuming a suppressed attack, etc.

These elements may belong to sets of equivalent priority; this means that they are all produced at once by a set of operations which may be considered a compound operation. The conditions for this are difficult to specify exactly; typically the new elements are all of the same length, but this is not essential. The main point is that the new elements are mutually supporting in some sense, that each makes sense only by virtue of the set. Examples are the E's in mm.5, 6, and 7 of Chopin's 1st prelude (if they are introduced separately, irrelevant rhythmic features result), or the notes in various voices of a 'zug.' The vagueness of this concept does not matter because it is not very important. This is because the compound can always be broken into its elements, and these must obey the rules of the system even though they may not make much sense beyond that (e.g., in the Chopin case the operations are on D's attached at each measure—if otherwise the separate nb. operations would not obey the rules of meter).

Elements, however, may be jointly introduced in a more basic and simple sense, viz. that the same operation produces them. Thus suspension produces a pair of tones (which replaces another pair with a different rhythm).

This concept distinguishes the new displacement (the resolution) from that part of the original tone of that pitch which occupied the same time-span. But this may well be considered futile; it may be argued that they are the same entity, the fact that one has an attack at its beginning and not the other being merely a consequence of the relational nature of attack (i.e., the fact that a different pitch, or a slight gap, precedes)—or at least that they are 'the same' to the extent that the system need not distinguish them. In this case we can say that the suspension-operation introduces only one new element; however it converts what was previously a non-element into an element as well, so that there are in any case two new elements, although one 'existed' already as a part of an element.

If however, we regard the subdivision of the displacement as a separate operation prior to suspension, then there is only one new element. But this will generally not be advisable; and besides it merely means that the two new elements are considered to be produced by two operations.

An element created by an operation (in the sense that it was not even part of a replaced element) may be called a proper element. Similarly, an element destroyed by an operation might be called a negative proper element if it previously existed as an element and not merely as part of one. In this sense suspension produces one proper element and destroys an improper negative element (i.e., any part of an element).

Now it can perhaps be generalized that the various operations of the system never destroy whole elements, but only parts of such; i.e., there are no negative proper elements.

An element may still be wholly suppressed, of course; but not until it has first been replaced by one including at least part of itself and something beyond that.

This view is probably tenable only if octaves can be considered single elements; but there seems no reason to object to that. [Alternatively we may simply reformulate the rule to say that only octave transfer can involve negative proper elements.] On the other hand, tones related by mixture must be separate elements; but then the rule of non-total-suppression will probably stand up (e.g., we do not usually consider a C-sharp as passing from a totally suppressed C-natural, and I think this will never be necessary).

[The difference between octaves and repeated notes is that with the former there is no analogously related entity as tied notes with the latter. Thus octaves can always be divided into their component pitches, whereas a long note is not necessarily significantly divisible into temporal parts; on the other hand, octaves can merge into "one sound" in a way that repeated tones cannot, and a tone can be so vague as to register in a way that it cannot as to time.]

An operation does not necessarily suppress anything, nor does it necessarily add anything new (it may only suppress). Indeed, it is arguable that the addition and suppression aspects of an operation can always be regarded as separate operations, and that these do not stand in any more definite relation to one another than operations belonging to an equivalent-priority set.

An operation can always be identified by what it adds and/or suppresses. For example a suspension adds a new predisplacement. However, it is not always unambiguous what new predisplacement is added (i.e., where it begins.)

This tempts us to consider the operation as essentially indistinguishable from the accented nb.; i.e., the fact that it is a suspension is a question of what equivalent-priority set it belongs to, or something of that sort. Specifically, it is plausible that an accented-nb. operation be called a suspension if and only if there is a higher-priority tone of the same pitch occupying a time-span ending where it begins. The 'only if' part here is indisputable, but perhaps this condition is not sufficient. We may add the further condition that no higher-priority tone of another pitch should occupy such a time-span (where higher-priority strictly implies displacement, etc.), however; this then seems at least close to conclusive.

This means that we must after all accept parts of tones as elements; but this is perhaps not harmful, provided we do not conclude that all possible parts of tones are elements. A part of a tone is an element if it is the whole segment produced by an operation, and only in that case. It follows of course that even the foreground elements are not automatically decidable; however, all foreground elements are parts of 'actual' tones (though some such parts are not elements).

The most essential aspect of an operation, then, is just the new elements it produces and/or suppresses. But if the new elements are the only criteria, then the various operations are all indistinguishable. This perhaps does not really matter, provided we can reconstruct 'inessential' definitions of them as we did for suspensions. In these definitions we make use of the superior–inferior relation, which can be reduced to a next-in-order relation (even though the order is only 'partial,' nextness is still clear).

In this approach, various matters become clearer. For example, an element cannot be inferior to part of itself. An entire tone is not necessarily an element, but if it is, then any part of itself must apparently be inferior to it.

Both the pitch and time-span of an element are characteristic of it; we do not consider 'change of time span' as an operation on an element, but this is no problem because these operations are no longer 'on' anything anyway. What were formerly 'operands' are here sets of elements satisfying certain conditions of priority.

1. The operation can be described in the first place as determined by what is added and subtracted, i.e., what *changes* are made.

As an example: in Op.111, m.2, we assume a full measure of FD/DB at some stage. Now the ambiguity here is whether the first change is to delay F/D (and suppress the last quarter of D/B), or to substitute E/C for FD/DB for the last half-note. In the latter case the F/D is a substitution of E/C; in the former case E/C substitutes for D/B.

Now this last question seems in a sense spurious; i.e., it seems to make no essential difference whether E/C substitutes for FD/DB or just for D/B. This can be explained, however, as follows: when F/D is given an attack at beat 3, it need not at the same stage have its attack at beat 1 suppressed. It can in fact be suppressed in beat 2 when E/C is introduced. The suppression at beat 1, after all, is not particularly associated with the introduction of F at beat 3, any more than with the introduction of F in beat 2 of m.1. Moreover, conversely if E/C is introduced prior to F/D, it still may be only a substitute for D/B in that the suppression at beat 1 may be prior to this.

So we see that the two analyses are actually the same with respect to what may be assumed to exist during beat 2 when E/C is introduced.

However, this example shows that this identity is not a proof that the analyses are really the same, even with respect to the sense of E/C; i.e., it shows that what exists with priority *in* the time-span of the element introduced is not particularly more decisive than what exists with priority in certain other time-spans (especially adjacent ones). Indeed, it may even be *less* decisive; for as we have seen, it makes little difference for the meaning of E/C whether F in beat 2 was immediately prior; it makes more difference whether F in beat 3 was prior. However, this refers only to *immediate* priority.

But of course there was in any case no reason to think that this *would* be a proof of identity. We assume, in general, that analyses are the same only if *all* their assertions of priority are the same.

2. We have seen that the question of what a given element *replaces* may be undecideable; this is because the suppression of elements of a harmony and the introduction of elements linearly next to them are really independent operations, although they may be associated as having 'equivalent priority.' Thus for an adequate description we must break the operations down still further. The new element does not 'replace' an element in the same time-span any more decisively than it replaces an element in certain other time-spans.

For example, the 'suspension' is a compound consisting of several factors:

1. The introduction of a new element S.
2. The partial or total suppression (optional!) of another element R which is superior to S and occupies a time-span beginning with S's and extending *further* than S's.
3. An element P of the same pitch as S, with a time-span ending the beginning of S; this element (which again may be totally or partially suppressed) must, again, be superior to S.

But the point is that in order to establish that S is a suspension it is not necessary to fix on *unique* elements P and R to which it stands in these relations.

A further question which arises is whether any such elements must be in any sense *immediately* prior to S. This seems to be so in the sense that they must not be suppressed with higher priority (though they *may* be suppressed with equivalent-priority).

Similarly the passing tone is defined with reference to superior elements in time spans adjacent to it (steps from it in pitch).

Can a tone then be a passing tone and also a suspension? For this to occur, there must be tone of step-related *and* identical pitches in the adjacently preceding time-span, neither one suppressed with higher priority. In other words, at some stage there must be a step-simultaneity. But this is perfectly possible: G-F-G-F-E might be so interpreted, provided the second F is attacked, which we may add as condition for being a passing tone.

3. Thus the essentials of a reductive analysis seem to be: we have a number of *elements* (tones and parts of tones) which are introduced, and possibly also suppressed, in a certain kind of partial order or pseudo-hierarchy. The order obeys certain rules which result in every element being a passing tone, neighbor, suspension, etc., etc. This order is determined by two relations, *priority* and *equality* (or; 'equivalent priority'); we need two relations, apparently, because non-ordering does not determine equality. It still may be possible to reduce these to one primitive, however.

The order itself has a complex structure which we are not certain of. E.g., it is clear that there must be initial elements, but far from clear that there must be asymmetry. (If this last condition is not necessary, then the definitions of 'passer,' etc., must be more complicated, and we shall need some new terms.) Other obvious conditions are: every foreground tone must be part of a second-element in the priority relation (unless it is an initial element, as e.g. in the case of pieces having a constant pedal-point); the initial elements are all *equal*; etc.

4. We now have to ask what is the *meaning* of 'priority.' The answer seems to be that though syntactically primitive, this term is not directly interpretable; i.e., it is a 'theoretical construct.' In that case it must appear in some lawlike conditionals; but this seems only true in a very complicated way. For example, the statement that some piece is part of the field of a priority relation in which every element is a passer, neighbor, etc., is notoriously weak, even possibly tautologous. To make it less so a great number of additional statements must be added; e.g., that all *equal* elements also satisfy various other conditions, etc. For example, it could be true that all suspensions are resolved, i.e., the R in the definition is never totally suppressed; or this could be true except in the case where the S is a particular pitch; and so on.

The laws involving priority are different in different pieces. *General* laws can perhaps be set up, but then it would be argued that these accomplish nothing except to decide, partly, what 'priority' means. For example we would perhaps refuse to consider a pair to be instances of priority if the first element is a proper part of the second.

In any event no proof that any element is prior to any other element seems available. Yet this goal is surely desirable. E.g., it ought to be possible to prove that a regular-rhythmed *Ursatz* has in a certain sense only one legitimate reduction (to one chord). This would not necessarily involve ruling out integration 'of' such a passage in all contexts, but only in ordering them as to preferability *prima facie*, so that if there is *no* context this order is decisive.

5. A more urgent question is: just what is it that we would like to have a proof for here? Consider the example C/E–G/D–C/C in equal quarter notes. Presumably we want the result that $C/G/C/E = \,\downarrow\,$ are initial elements. It might seem that we also want the result that the G/D are inferior to the other foreground tones, but this is not so clear; i.e., this may only be required in the sense that they are not 'remnants' of superior elements which have been partially suppressed. However, we certainly want the result that D is a passing tone, and this seems to require at least the attack of C at the end of D's time-span (although it does not require any other difference from the set of initial elements); similarly the final bass C should be demonstrably superior to the preceding G, since G/D and C/C should be equality sets.

This is perhaps all that is absolutely necessary; the 'superiority' of C/E to G/D may follow from its being the initial remnant of a superior chord. The various suppressions necessary to reach the actual piece may be considered unordered. G/D are the terminal elements; C/C are intermediary; the foreground C/E are not elements at all, but remnants of initial elements.

In practice usually more than this is asserted. For example the suppressions of at least the outer I tones are considered *equal* to the introduction of the V tones.[7] Beyond this, it is also usual to consider the introductions of the final C's to be equal to the suppression of the part of the initial E occupying that time-span, and also the suppression of the part of the upper C occupying the first and second beats. These further assertions give the priority order the additional structural feature that every element is prior, equal, or inferior to every other element both with regard to its introduction and its suppression; indeed we usually assume that this holds for all elements in overlapping time-spans (perhaps with occasional exceptions). They also have several other effects. For example, they yield a sense in which we can *deny* the D is a nb., and a more specific meaning to the notions of *arpeggiation* applied to C/G and C/E/.

But these assertions differ from the rest in that their proof involves essentially the notion of the rhythmic weakness of the V beat compared to the final beat. If we change the rhythm to half-note/eighth-note/dotted-quarter-note ♩ ♪♩. , for example, these aspects of the analysis would be different; the others would remain, except that the final C's would become remnants (i.e., the *elements* of the analysis would be essentially the same).

This difference is unclear because change of rhythm affects elementhood as well as order. However, there is a clearer difference: the first set of assertions said nothing about the *order of suppressions*. It may be just this that characterizes them as the *essential* assertions.

This seems to be true; yet we must notice that the 'inessential' assertions also had a very definite affect on the application of usual terms such as nb., arpeggiation, etc.

It follows that it is of interest to set up a group of terms which are defined on the basis of *essential* relations only.

---

[7] Also the G in beat 1's suppression is considered equal to G's introduction in beat 2; and G's suppression in beat 3 probably equal to these

In this connection we note that arpeggiation can only be defined if suppression is recognized; yet it may well be that it does not make any difference at what stage the suppression occurs. Thus an interval could be said to be an arpeggiation if and only if it consists of remnants of a simultaneity. A remnant here is anything the whole of which does not occur in the foreground.

To see whether it is really necessary to consider the order of suppression at all, we reconsider a case where much use was made of this (Beethoven's A-flat sonata).

Adagio molto.

The argument here was that the top C in m.1 was a suspension of a suppressed C; but nevertheless the B-flat in m.3 passed from A-flat and did *not* nb. to C. Thus it seemed that there must be no such C at m.1 at the stage at which m.3's B-flat was introduced, although there was one, of course, in the extreme background; yet there must again be one (introduced by coupling) at the stage at which m.1's B-flat was introduced. Since this B-flat is much more local than the other one, it was therefore assumed that there must be a double introduction and suppression.

Now this, be it noted, depended on the premise that the larger B-flat was to be introduced before the local one. The reason for this assumption was not merely that it was larger, however (which would clearly be insufficient), but that it corresponded in sequence to the opening A-flat; thus by this means the introduction in mm.1 and 3 could be considered *equal*, as suggested by their sequential relation. Thus we see that the need for considering order of suppressions is related to the notion of *equality* and possibly only arises out of the use of that notion. Otherwise in the present case, for example, we could consider the 1st B-flat prior to the 2nd, and hence only one suppression of the opening C would be needed.

This way of looking at the passage foregoes any connection between size and priority, however; moreover the loss of the notion of equality may well be serious. For these and other reasons this way out is probably untenable.

However, there was another premise involved too, viz.: that if the opening C were not yet suppressed, the B-flat in m.3 would have to be regarded as a lower nb. This is not too convincing.

But what is harder to get around is that if the opening C is not suppressed when it is introduced, the C at m.5 is not an arpeggiation in any very clear sense.

Even this is not very convincing. There is, as suggested before, still the point that the opening C is essentially suppressed (a point which could also be used to deny that B-flat is a lower nb.).

All this suggests that a more critical case would arise if we had an *actually present tone* which was said to have been introduced, suppressed, and then reintroduced. I.e., the question is: is it possible to find such a case, in which it is necessary for some reason to have the tone absent at some prior stage (though present again at a still prior one).

Consider only mm.1–2. Then perhaps the C actually in m.1 is an example of this. This C would normally be considered (1) to belong to the background C as a part; (2) to be suppressed equal with the introduction of B-flat; (3) to be reintroduced as a suspension, equal with the suppression of 3/4 of the B-flat.

The point of this is that otherwise at some stage C and B-flat occur simultaneously; i.e., this is so if the introduction of B-flat does not involve the suppression of C, and also so if vice versa. Hence the step-displacement here is indistinguishable from an arpeggiation (unless perhaps by the nonoccurrence of B-flat *at the beginning of the whole measure*, at any level). Even so, it could be argued that this distinction is *eventually* made by suppression the B-flat in the dotted-quarter and the C in the last eighth. Also it could be argued that if the B-flat were never suppressed, the C would still be a suspension here; for this purpose it suffices to suppress the last eighth of the C—and perhaps not even this is strictly necessary, as some instrumental division might clarify the C–B-flat notion even if C were also repeated. Only the re-attack of B-flat is clearly and absolutely essential; the reason being that otherwise nothing defines an *end* to C before the end of the measure (a rest would be insufficient).

But all this only shows that the suppression-order is perhaps not necessary to determine whether there is a suspension; it does not show that we don't need this order for other reasons.

For example, in m.1 there is an inner C. Once the upper C has been suppressed, we may need this inner C in order to justify the upper one's re-introduction by coupling. Thus the use of the order of suppressions could be explanatory for the inner C (although of course in this case there is better reason for it anyway, viz. the following D-flat).

What all this comes down to is that indeed the suppressions can all be left to the extreme foreground if we are willing to allow the middleground a certain kind of (avoidable!) incoherence. But one could on the same ground leave all rhythmic or register assignments to the foreground, for example. In general, the advantages of assigning order to the suppressions are the same as for the introductions. Moreover, insofar as equality is relevant, equality of an introduction and a suppression is often the clearest and most obvious kind, because of its maintenance of the same *number* of tones in a passage.

To the introduction of a new element there corresponds an inverse process of 'reduction.' The usual 'remainder after reduction' consists of *some* superior elements in the time-span neighborhood of the omitted element, enough to determine, e.g., that it is a passing tone, etc.

For example the V chord in m.1 of the *Pathetique* slow movement [Beethoven Op.13, II] can be omitted in a reduction of m.1 + m.2's attack. This is the simplest kind possible, omission of a set of pure weak passing tones. The reduction simply extends m.1's first chord over the whole measure, and the reduced passage appears as an arpeggiation of treble and bass.

Similarly the V in m.2 can be omitted in a reduction to 1+ measure. But there is a difference here in that the bass G is then an unprepared nb. It substitutes for an A-flat in another register in this case, at best. This complication does not arise if the V is omitted only in a 2+ measure reduction; but this can only be done if the proposed reduction of m.1 is done first—i.e., it has to be shown that the preceding 1½ measure can all be regarded as one chord, for the purpose. (Also then the inner B-flat is a nb., not a passer from C.)

At the same time it must be observed that in this case two sets of passers are introduced with different rhythms; ♩♩ in one case and ♩.♩

in the other; whereas if m.2 is reduced without reference to m.1 the two rhythms are the same.

This consequence could be avoided by supposing that the 2nd V was originally introduced *at* m.2 and delayed subsequently; but there would still be some difference in the processes leading to the V's, and there seems no advantage in this.

It could also be pointed out that in order to give m.2's beginning a root-position chord, i.e., A-flat/C in the registers of the beginning, it is not necessary to omit the V in m.1; it is only necessary to 'reduce' m.1 in the sense of 'omitting' the suppression of these tones. In that case, however, the suppressions at m.2 are subsequent to the introduction in m.1, which seems to remove the rationale for the passing tones in m.1. But more convincingly: this seems reasonable only because the V in m.1 *is* inferior to this I.

Another argument would be that once the V in m.1 is omitted, the beginning is an arpeggiation and the opening C undisplaced, and thus the second V can be reduced out without implying that the beginning of m.2 has already been reduced out. This is perhaps the same as saying that the V in m.2 can be derived at a stage where m.2 is simply repeating m.1 (except for the addition of the high E-flat and the inner C); i.e., it comes *between* the additions and suppressions which constitute the arpeggiation of m.1. It would then be clear that this V is unordered with m.2; but it would also be clear that it is superior to the other V (unless vice versa, which is out of the question).

But all this manipulation seems a bad idea, in that part of the point of allowing a reduction to m.2 alone is to allow that the sense of G as a 'transferred nb.' and B-flat as a nb. to two A-flats, is also a valid sense of the second half of m.2; and also to provide a sense in which this V is *not* superior to the other one.

Still, it is an interesting point that the superiority of the second V depends on the ordering of suppressions; the reason being, moreover, merely that unless it is considered superior its derivation is more complicated.

But now notice that these same arguments can in general be used to force a much more definite superiority order. Suppose we have an eight-measure phrase based on I followed by a (no longer) passage based on V. Now in order to derive the large V, the eight measures must be reduced to one chord (or at least a repeated chord). I.e., once the opening I has been elaborated, it no longer serves as a proper origin for the large V.

Put similarly, in general in the case of interruptions, thus: E-D-E-D-C, it can be argued that if the 1st D is a passing tone, it must be superior to the 2nd, because the second descent must be de-arpeggiated in order to provide a C at the right rhythmic point. As a matter of fact, I usually get around this precisely by assuming that the attack of the C under the 2nd E does not occur *with* the arpeggiation of the 2nd half. But here this assumption seems harmless because the 2nd D does not substitute for C, but E.

In the case of C/E–[D–C/(E)]–D–C, on the other hand, assumption that the second E is not suppressed with the initial arpeggiation is insufficient; it must also remain unsuppressed when the first D is introduced, and this seems less reasonable.

To put the *Pathetique* case another way, the reduction of m.2 independently of m.1 is *possible*, and yields senses for the V tones similar to those they have if m.1–2 are reduced as a whole. To get the most clear and simple meanings for these tones, however, m.1–2 must be considered as a whole and thus the second V considered superior to the 1st. Thus in this particular case this reduction is 'preferable,' though the other is not irrelevant.

The ambiguity even here, then, is more distinct than the ambiguity as to which elaborations should be considered prior of, for example, the arpeggiations within the halves of m.1. The reason is that this really makes no difference at all, since the time-spans *concerned* are completely discrete. In the question we have been considering, the possible orders resulted in different *justificatory* time-spans even though the time-spans of the introductions themselves are completely discrete.

Thus the most trivial kind of ambiguity is of the order of introductions with discrete relevant time-spans. Less trivial is the ambiguity of order of introduction with discrete introduction-spans but overlapping relevance-spans. In the former case we consider the 'ambiguity' to merely reflect an error in assuming serial total order of introductions, in that which order is assumed makes no difference.

In the latter case it makes a slight difference; it determines whether the second half of m.2 is rhythmically simpler or simpler in pitch relations. One order is probably 'preferable' in some sense.

It could also be said that this ambiguity too reflects an error; in considering the order of suppressions equally significant with the order of introductions. Or perhaps in assuming that an introduction has a unique relevance-span. The ambiguity resulting is slight in that in any case the sense of the V tones are similar, i.e., they substitute for I tones. If the suppressions are all left to the foreground, they can even be said to substitute for the same tones. Moreover (as not noticed before), this could be said in any case if we consider the A♭/C from m.1 to be reintroduced at m.2 only to be suppressed again.

Perhaps this sort of maneuver should be forbidden by a rule of some sort. It would be allowed, however, if the reintroduced C were then suspended, for example (as we have seen here in the A-flat sonata). Indeed this seems to be a case already noted: the 'totally suppressed' tone.

In that case we are left with the idea of leaving the suppression to the foreground again.

(Another ambiguity is the question of whether m.2's D♭ results from suspension, or from the division directly into ♩.♪, or simply from a ♩♩ division. The decision between the last two is a cast of substitution for the same tone and would seem almost completely trivial; however, it seems best to avoid the third possibility because (1) E♭ is not repeated, and (2) this destroys the relation to the D♭ in m.1. The first possibility seems contraindicated by the relative consonance of the E♭ with the bass G, etc. The second therefore seems best, and one may question whether this is an ambiguity at all. As in the case of the V tones, however, the *possibility* of the other derivations remains.)

Notice that leaving the suppressions to the foreground (or considering the unordered) is equivalent to considering that a reducible passage need not be reduced to provide the proper 'justification' for an introduction. Or rather, the noteworthy point here is the converse of that. Also there is still another equivalent formulation of the same notion, viz., that a remnant of a superior element can serve this purpose—even if, as in the present case, it is a non-adjacent (in time) remnant.

The effect of this principle would merely be to make the priority order more ambiguous. We have seen that this is a doubtful virtue. The conclusion that seems indicated is that it is useful to distinguish priority as indicated, even in view of this principle, from priority as indicated if it is dropped, without adopting (or rejecting) the principle.

Thus our attitude here is different from our attitude to ambiguities produced by insistence on a serial order of derivation; that we regard as just an error.

PART 3

The Contents of the Winham Archive

Godfrey Winham's writings on music divide physically into three classes, the first comprising loose sheets gathered together in a series of folders and designated by the notation "*_," the second comprising intact spiral-bound notebooks and designated by the notation "N_," and the third comprising material given on score paper (mostly musical notation, yet with some explanatory notes) and designated by the notation "S_." (The musical notations are not transcribed but xeroxed: the accompanying text is transcribed.) The material in the first category (the loose folders) is written in pencil on sheets of lined notebook paper. According to the editor, most of these loose pages were gathered (and at times collated) by Winham himself, and were found sometimes in a separate box, or in a single pile, or in an envelope. (It is obvious, for example, the material of *79 was gathered with the intention of using it as the raw material for a book on the application of the logical disciplines to the elementary questions of music theory.) Some of these folders, however, contain material which Roger Maren himself found in notebooks devoted to nonmusical subjects and subsequently removed. The manuscripts on score paper comprise both notebooks and groups of pages gathered together by Winham.

The manuscripts and their transcriptions are further divided among sixteen archival boxes, holding respectively 1) *1a–*23f; 2) *24a–*43; 3) *44a–*80; 4) *1a–*23 (transcribed); 5) *24a–*39f (transcribed); 6) *40–*80 (transcribed); 7) N1–N11; 8) N12–N22; 9) N23–N32; 10) N33–N43; 11) N1–N17 (transcribed); 12) N18–N30 (transcribed); 13) N31–N43 (transcribed); 14) S1–S18; 15) S19–S31; and 16) S1–31 (xeroxed and transcribed). (This division is pragmatically important in that the Special Collections allow access only to a single box at any given time, and the distribution of material is nowhere given in the catalog or on the boxes themselves.) The first box also contains a copy of James Randall's unpublished *Tonality* and Roger Maren's editorial notes as contained in the volume *Godfrey Winham's Unpublished Writings on Music*.

Both a descriptive table of contents and a comprehensive index are given in this introductory volume. Insomuch as there is a real freshness in Maren's descriptions of the contents of the archive, I have only slightly altered this material, correcting several obvious typographical errors, preserving most of the orthography of the original. The table of contents is preceded by several explanatory notes. "(Inc.)" means that the item breaks off abruptly and obviously. Either Winham intended to go back to it and could not find it or was sidetracked, or the continuation is lost. "(J)" means that the item is a jumble, and there is no evidence that he even attempted to put the material in coherent form. "(NR)" means that the transcription has not been proofread. "(ADT)" refers to the sets of axioms, definitions, and theorems that Godfrey Winham developed over the years in his attempt to axiomatize the tonal system.

In addition, the manuscripts contain compositional notes for several of Winham's completed pieces. These include *Composition for Orchestra* [1962], ed. Jacques-Louis Monod (Ship Bottom, New Jersey: Association for the Promotion of New Music, 1984); *The Habit of Perfection* [Soprano and string quartet, 1956] (Ship Bottom, New Jersey: Association for the Promotion of New Music, 1982); *To Prove My Love: Three Sonnets of Shakespeare* [soprano and piano] (*Perspectives of New Music* 13/2, Spring–Summer 1975, 67–83); a tonal piece that is probably the *Sonata for Orchestra* (Ship Bottom, New Jersey: Association for the Promotion of New Music, 1982); and *Variations on a Theme by James Pierpont for Piano* [1973] (Ship Bottom, New Jersey: Association for the Promotion of New Music, 1982). The occasional references to a work initialed "NP" may be a misreading of "HP," in other words, *The Habit of Perfection*.

Maren, for obvious reasons, does not supply a table of contents for the material on score paper (although he supplies a very comprehensive index). In order to give an accurate representation of the nature of the archive (and in particular to emphasize the depth and breadth of Winham's engagement with actual music rather than simply with theoretical constructs) I have reconstructed a partial table of contents from Maren's index. This table indicates only those places where he is sketching identified or identifiable pieces. These identifications were made by Roger Maren, Bethany Winham, and Arthur Komar. Much of the remainder of this material consists of compositional sketching, contrapuntal and fugal exercises, and places where he works out some of his theoretical ideas in notation. In addition to the works cited in the previous paragraph, we find compositional sketches for a *Cello Piece for Phil*, a *Fugue in C minor*, and several untitled pieces: we may assume that none of these reached completion.

The table of contents reads as follows.

Table of Contents, *Godfrey Winham's Unpublished Writings on Music*

*19	Notes for talk on variation, ambiguity, Schenker, and Beethoven Op. 109 (Inc.)	4
*20a	*Habit of Perfection*—mostly list of aggregates (Inc.)	2
b	Notes on *HP* (Inc.)	11
*21a	Criteria of closure in the line	1
b	Schoenberg *Violin Concerto;* set forms and odds and ends (J)	24
c	Notes on duration sets	2
d	Note on pitch-structure in 12-tone system (Inc.)	2
e	Note on why anyone cares if a piece is tonal (Inc.)	1
*22a	Description of analytical sketch of Beethoven Op. 23	4
b	Note on rhythm of first twenty measures of Mozart *Quintet*, K. 515	1
c	Note on *An Sylvia*	1
d	Note on Brahms *Symphony No. 2*	1
e	School paper on Tristan, Act I	13
f	School paper on opera	16
*23a	Scales, tendencies (J)	2
b	Scales, tendencies (J)	10
c	Genesis of major and minor scales (Inc.)	3
d	Table of contents and preface to book on theory of music (Inc.)	2
e	Suggestion of array composition technique (Inc.)	1
f	On Stravinsky	2
*24a	Boulez, Perle, Babbitt on Schoenberg, and attack on post-Webernism	30
b	On a symphony (J)	2
c	On being a reactionary	2
d	Critical comments on Schoenberg's rhythm	1
e	Nature and function of musical systems	2
f	Cone's "Conversations with Sessions" (Inc.)	5
*25a	Notes for lecture on Schenker and ambiguity (Inc.)	6
b	Tonality and temporal order	2
c	Explanation of analytical sketches of Mozart K. 331	4
d	Comments on various of his own theories of tonality (J)	56
e	On staff notation and scales (for nonmusicians)	6
*26a	Explanation of unfound example	4
b	Analysis of measures 58–64 of unidentified piece	3

c	Dynamics (Inc.)	2
d	Pitch class, interval (Inc.)	7
e	Dynamics, time (Inc.)	4
f	Problem of structure	3
g	Concept of attack	8
h	What is musical analysis?	8
i	Plausibility of logico-mathematical music theory	2
j	Structure	6
k	Language form for analysis and possibility of formalization	13
l	Congruence transformations	3
m	Logical basis, range of variables, general program, etc.	7
n	Justification of enterprise (J)	7
o	Analysis vs. description; numerical values, and musicology (J)	6
p	Significance; octave equivalence (J)	3
q	Impossibility of characterizing pitch qualities via "tonal function"	3
r	General theory of musical phenomena; analysis, history, and value	3
s	Formulation of part–whole system; metric for phenomenal and abstract space	16
t	Pitch-predicates	3
u	Pitch, dynamics, attack, and timbre (J)	6
v	Abstract of the whole work	4
w	Metaterminology (Inc.)	11
x	?	6
y	?	4
z	Terminology	1

*80	Analysis of *Dichterliebe*, Op. 48, No. 2	11

*81	Untyped, unedited axioms, definitions, and theorems

N1	(Mostly work stimulated by J. K. Randall's *Tonality*)
1–28	Notes to self on Randall's *Tonality*
29–31	Temporal asymmetry, memory, time, and musical analysis
32–35	More on Randall-scale, root, fifth, and normal form
36–38	On what would constitute a theory of basic tonality
39–43	The chord; harmonic series generation of triads, etc.
44–92	Scales, modes, and tendencies
93–97	Inversion of harmonic intervals
98–104	Phrygian mode
105–115	Alteration, tonicization
116–118	J. K. Randall's *Tonality*
119–159	Scales, modes, tendencies, and Randall's *Tonality*

N2

N3

N4

N5

N10 (insert)
1–13   Fundamental theory of concordance
14–95 More on concordance

N11
1–6   Consecutive fifths
7–8   *Dichterliebe No. 1* analysis
9–14   *Dichterliebe No. 2* analysis
15   Key of *Dichterliebe No. 1*
16–18 More on *Dichterliebe No. 2*
19   C# in *Dichterliebe No. 1*
20–41 Analysis of *Tristan* prelude
42–50 *Dichterliebe No. 4*
51–75 Dialog on tonal music, especially scales, modulation, tonicization, and chromatic alteration
76–80 Dialog on analysis, especially concept of suppression
81–87 Continuation from p. 41 on *Tristan* prelude

N12
1   Interruption
2–4   Beethoven Op. 109
5–6   Tendencies; support
7   Examination questions for class

N13
1–5   Chopin *Nocturne,* Op. 15, No. 2 and Beethoven Op. 26 (analytical discussion)
6   Paragraph about one of the variations in his piece *Pierpont Variations*
7–10   On reduction and tonal operations
11   On interruption
12–18 On analytical sketching and metrical analysis, especially *Well Tempered Clavier*, Prelude I
19–21 On Komar's analytical remarks on Chopin *Prelude No. 1*
22–24 On tonal operations and sketching, especially Chopin *Prelude No. 1*
26–29 Analysis of *Dichterliebe No. 1*

N14
1–11   On formalization problems (structure, similarity)
12–17 Definitions of "music theory," "work," and discussion of subject matter of tonal theory
18–21 More definition of field
22–47 Tonal operations and analytical sketching
48–49 History of the present tonal theory

16–17   Inspiration vs. conscious construction
18–21   Replication in array composition
22–25   Rhythmic canons in *Composition for Orchestra*
26–31   Early drafts of Ph.D. thesis with (29ff) history of his own 12-tone development
32–33   On instrumentation

N19

1, 2   Description vs. analysis
3–10   Significance and formalized language
11   Brief note on methodology and "universes" or geometrical spaces
12–26   Description vs. analysis
27–36   "Musical Works" as phenomena vs. physical events
37–50   Semiotic applied to music, need for language base
51   "Musical Work" again
53–54   Analysis defined and discussed
55–57   Musical work and structure discussed
58–66   *Principia Mathematica*, Quine
67–76   Better draft of semiotic (37ff) and justification of program
77–120   More on formal languages; many logical statements, Russell's Paradox
121–124   Conditions for a language in which analysis can be expressed
125–138   More logic and formalization
139–152   Outline (abstract) of analytical work, definitions, and remarks
153–156   Abstract of semiotical study of musical scores
157–168   Logical problems
169–184   Total inversion of tonal works; harmonic relations
185–209   Various notes on musico-logical problems
210–214   On tonal music as basis for musical education and purpose of theory
215–222   Temporal relations
223–224   Dynamics

N20

1–28   Roots, octave equivalents, and harmonic series
29–102   Theories of harmonic quality and concordance
103–105   Criticism of Randall's definitions in *Tonality*
106–163   More on theories of concordance, roots, etc.
164   On Berg's music

N21

1–2   Notes on Beethoven Op. 27, No. 2
3–4   Outline of course on discrete-time sound analysis and synthesis
5   Trivial note on apparent directionality of loudspeaker sound

N24
1–3	Notes on *Moonlight Sonata* and Op. 26 sonata of Beethoven
4–6	Retrogression's effect on structure
7–11	Notes to sketches, probably of his *Pierpont Variations*
12	On Beethoven Op. 27, No. 2
13–19	On sketches of Beethoven Op. 2, No. 2
20	On Bach *Well Tempered Clavier*, Book I, Prelude II
21–22	Arpeggiation
23–26	Suspension
27	Definition of Urlinie (basic line)
28–30	Bach *Well Tempered Clavier*, Book I, Prelude I

N25
1–5	Relevance to tonal theory of tone–overtone relations
6–38	Notes and disjointed comments on definitions and explications of basic terms of tonal theory

N26   On description as opposed to analysis of music

N27
1	Outline of book of music criticism
2–9	Notes on "The Intentional Fallacy" from *The Verbal Icon* (Wimsatt & Beardsley)
10–13	Notes on Instrumentation
14–28	Incomplete essay on 12-tone music and its composition
29	Outline of five essays on composition
30	Summary of "The Situation" in music criticism and discourse
31–36	Notes on a theory of rhythm
37	Instrumentation
38	Schoenberg: summary of "periods"
39–46	Notes on instrumentation for orchestra piece
47	Outline of work on musical meaning
48–49	Notes on some piece
50–53	Rules for strict harmonic counterpoint
54–56	On Richard's "Practical Criticism"
57–59	On Reti's *Thematic Process in Music*
60–63	Instrumentation
64–66	Notes on advertising as root-problem in U.S. society
67–69	On competence, genius, and mature spontaneity in composing
70–72	On Keller's *Functional Analysis*

N28
1–13	Temporal asymmetry, memory, and time (F)
14–19	Attributes of sense-data (F)

8–15   Informal outline of array composition at an early stage
16–17   Letter to Allen Forte on array composition
18–30   More formal work on array composition

N43   (Possibly all course notes)
1–11   Preliminary notes for tonal theory course
12–22   More of the same with emphasis on *stability*
23   On minor scales
24–26   Tonal system as outside composition, analysis based
 on abstraction
27   Notes on Chopin *Prelude in C minor*
28–41   Attempt at defining tonal system
42–56   On tonal operations, operands, and resultants
57–85   More of the same but mostly on change of scale

S1 2–4   Henry Weinberg, *Songs*
7–8   Ludwig van Beethoven, *Sonata*, Op. 109, II
9   Franz Schubert, *Sonata in A major*, Op. posth.
10   Franz Schubert, *Sonata in C minor*
14   Robert Schumann, *Piano Concerto*, Op. 54
17   Robert Schumann, *Dichterliebe*, Op. 48, No. 2

S2 1–3   Milton Babbitt, *Vision and Prayer*
4–7   W. A. Mozart, *Concerto in C major*, K. 467

S3 3   Benjamin Britten, *Spring Symphony*, Op. 44
4–5   Alban Berg, *Der Wein*

S4 6   Benjamin Britten, *Spring Symphony*, Op. 44
7   Robert Helps, *In Memoriam*

S5 1–5   Robert Schumann, *Dichterliebe*, Op. 48, No. 2
6   Robert Schumann, *Dichterliebe*, Op. 48, No. 1
7–10   Robert Schumann, *Dichterliebe*, Op. 48, No. 2
12   Robert Schumann, *Dichterliebe*, Op. 48, No. 2

S6 1–3   Friedrich Chopin, *Prelude No. 20* (C minor)
4   J. S. Bach, *Well Tempered Clavier*, Book I, Fugue II

S7 3   Ludwig van Beethoven, *Sonata*, Op. 14, No. 2
5   J. S. Bach, *Well Tempered Clavier*, Book I, Prelude II
7–9   W. A. Mozart, *Sonata in A minor*, K. 310
11–43   Ludwig van Beethoven, *Symphony No. 6*, I
45–47   Richard Wagner, *Tristan und Isolde*, Vorspiel
49–51   W. A. Mozart, *Symphony No. 40*, II

54–56 Johannes Brahms, *Intermezzo*, Op. 119, No. 1
57–60 Ludwig van Beethoven, *Sonata*, Op. 2, No. 2, II
61 Friedrich Chopin, *Prelude No. 20* (C minor)

S8
1–15 Richard Wagner, *Tristan und Isolde*, Vorspiel
16–18 Ludwig van Beethoven, *String Quartet*, Op. 132, Adagio
19 Johannes Brahms, *Chorale*, Op. 62, No. 7
20–26 Johannes Brahms, *Variations on a Theme* by Haydn
29 J. S. Bach, *Well Tempered Clavier*, Book I, Prelude I
36 Fugue in C minor
37–39 J. S. Bach, *Well Tempered Clavier*, Book I, Prelude I

S9
2 Robert Schumann, *Dichterliebe*, Op. 48, No. 1
4–7 Ludwig van Beethoven, *Sonata*, Op. 27, No. 2
9–13 Johannes Brahms, *Intermezzo*, Op. 119, No. 1
16 *Fugue in C minor*

S10
1–4a Ludwig van Beethoven, *Sonata*, Op. 109, II
6–9 Friedrich Chopin, *Prelude No. 20* (C minor)
10–19 Johannes Brahms, *Intermezzo*, Op. 119, No. 1

S11
1–3 W. A. Mozart, *Sonata in A major*, K. 331
6 W. A. Mozart, *Sonata in A major*, K. 331
8–9 W. A. Mozart, *Sonata in A major*, K. 331
11–14 W. A. Mozart, *Sonata in A major*, K. 331
18 Ludwig van Beethoven, *Sonata*, Op. 2, No. 2, II
19 Ludwig van Beethoven, *Sonata*, Op. 2, No. 3, II
20 Ludwig van Beethoven, *Sonata*, Op. 2, No. 3, III
26 W. A. Mozart, *Sonata in A major*, K. 331
30 Anton Bruckner, *Symphony No. 7*, I
32–34 Friedrich Chopin, *Nocturne in G-minor*, Op. 39, No. 1
40 Richard Wagner, *Tristan und Isolde*, Vorspiel
42–44 Arnold Schoenberg, *Quartet No. 4*
46–57 Benjamin Britten, *Noye's Fludde* (27–33)

S12 Friedrich Chopin, *Nocturne in G-minor*, Op. 39, No. 1
5–15 Friedrich Chopin, *Nocturne in G-minor*, Op. 39, No. 1
16 Friedrich Chopin, *Nocturne in F-major*, Op. 15, No. 1
24–30 Friedrich Chopin, *Nocturne in G-minor*, Op. 39, No. 1
34–40 Ludwig van Beethoven, *Sonata*, Op. 109, II
41 Friedrich Chopin, *Nocturne in G-minor*, Op. 39, No. 1

44–56   W. A. Mozart, *Sonata in A minor*, K. 310
57   W. A. Mozart, *Sonata in A major*, K. 331
58–59   W. A. Mozart, *Sonata in A minor*, K. 310
60   Johannes Brahms, *Variations on a Theme by Haydn*
62–63   Benjamin Britten, *Turn of the Screw*, Prologue to Act I
64   Malcolm Peyton, *Sonnet I* ("Musick to Heare")
69   Robert Schumann, *Dichterliebe*, Op. 48, No. 2
74   W. A. Mozart, *Sonata in A major*, K. 331
75   Arnold Schoenberg, *Das Buch der hängenden Gärten*

S13

S14
1–4   Ludwig van Beethoven, *Sonata*, Op. 27, No. 2
7–9   Ludwig van Beethoven, *Sonata*, Op. 2, No. 2, II
11   J. S. Bach, *Well Tempered Clavier*, Book I, Prelude II
16   *Pierpont Variations*

S15

S16
1   (Analytic sketches for unidentified piece in E major)
2   Friedrich Chopin, *Nocturne in G-minor*, Op. 39, No. 1

S17
1–7   Ludwig van Beethoven, *Sonata*, Op. 13 ("Pathetique")
8   (blank)
9   (unknown work for piano, F-sharp minor)
13–20   Arnold Schoenberg, *Herzgewächse*
21–32   (various studies of tonal operations, counterpoint)
33–35   *Pierpont Variations*

S18
1–3   Ludwig van Beethoven, *Sonata*, Op. 26
5   (unknown work)
7   Ludwig van Beethoven, *Sonata*, Op. 23 ("Waldstein"), I
9–10   Franz Schubert, *Sonata in C minor*
12   Ludwig van Beethoven, *Sonata*, Op. 23 ("Waldstein"), I
13–15   Franz Schubert, *Sonata in C minor*
16–21   Ludwig van Beethoven, *Sonata*, Op. 23 ("Waldstein"), I
25–27   Ludwig van Beethoven, *Sonata*, Op. 7, II
28   Ludwig van Beethoven, *Sonata*, Op. 2, No. 2, III
29–30   Ludwig van Beethoven, *Sonata*, Op. 2, No. 2, II
32–33   Ludwig van Beethoven, *Sonata*, Op. 2, No. 2, II
39   Friedrich Chopin, *Prelude No. 20* (C minor)
42   Ludwig van Beethoven, *Sonata*, Op. 109, II

S19

1	J. S. Bach, *Well Tempered Clavier,* Book I, Prelude II
3	Friedrich Chopin, *Prelude No. 9* (E-major)
4	J. S. Bach, *Well Tempered Clavier,* Book I, Fugue I
5	J. S. Bach, *Well Tempered Clavier,* Book I, Fugue II
6	J. S. Bach, Well Tempered Clavier, Book I, Fugue I
7	J. S. Bach, Well Tempered Clavier, Book I, Prelude I
8	Paul Hindemith, *Mathis der Maler*
12	J. S. Bach, *Well Tempered Clavier,* Book I, Fugue I
13	Friedrich Chopin, *Prelude No. 2* (A-minor)
14	Ludwig van Beethoven, *Sonata,* Op. 23 ("Waldstein"), II
15–17	Friedrich Chopin, *Prelude No. 9* (E-major)
19	Robert Schumann, *Dichterliebe,* Op. 48, No. 2
20	J. S. Bach, *Well Tempered Clavier,* Book I, Prelude I
21	J. S. Bach, *Well Tempered Clavier,* Book I, Prelude II
23	Benjamin Britten, *St. Nicholas,* VIII

S20

1	Ludwig van Beethoven, *Sonata,* Op. 23 ("Waldstein"), II
2	Ludwig van Beethoven, *Sonata,* Op. 23 ("Waldstein"), II
3	Friedrich Chopin, *Prelude No. 4* (E-minor); *Prelude No. 20* (C minor)
4	Friedrich Chopin, *Prelude No. 9* (E-major)
5	Friedrich Chopin, *Prelude No. 2* (A-minor)
6	Friedrich Chopin, *Prelude No. 4* (E-minor)
7	Ludwig van Beethoven, *Sonata,* Op. 23 ("Waldstein"), II
8	J. S. Bach, *Well Tempered Clavier,* Book I, Prelude II
9	J. S. Bach, *Well Tempered Clavier,* Book I, Prelude I
10	Ludwig van Beethoven, *Sonata,* Op. 14, No. 2

S21

1–3	Ludwig van Beethoven, *Symphony No. 3*
3	Ludwig van Beethoven, *Sonata,* Op. 14, No. 1
4	Leroy Anderson, *Syncopated Clock*
11	Arnold Schoenberg, *Quartet No. 4*
14–17	Arnold Schoenberg, *Quartet No. 4*

S22

5–7	Anton Bruckner, *Symphony No. 7,* I
7	J. S. Bach, *Mass in B minor,* "Domine Deus;" Beethoven, *Sonata,* Op. 27, No. 2
8–11	*Orchestra Piece*
12	*Habit of Perfection*
13–14	*Orchestra Piece*
17–18	Friedrich Chopin, *Prelude No. 20* (C minor)

20	Anton Bruckner, *Symphony No. 7*, II
25–26	*Cello Piece for Phil*
28–32	*Orchestra Piece*
42–46	Friedrich Chopin, *Prelude No. 20* (C minor)
47	Arnold Schoenberg, *Das Buch der hängenden Gärten*
48–49	Friedrich Chopin, *Prelude No. 20* (C minor)
50–65	*Orchestra Piece*
66	Robert Schumann, *Piano Concerto*, Op. 54
69–75	Richard Wagner, *Tristan und Isolde*, Vorspiel
76	Johannes Brahms, *Deutsche Volkslieder*, No. 14 ("Maria Ging")
77	Anton Bruckner, *Symphony No. 7*, I
78–80	Richard Wagner, *Tristan und Isolde*, Vorspiel
83–85	Ludwig van Beethoven, *Concerto for Piano No. 4*, Op. 58
86–88	Johannes Brahms, *Deutsche Volkslieder*, No. 14 ("Maria Ging")
89	Ludwig van Beethoven, *Concerto for Piano No. 4*, Op. 58
90	Franz Schubert, Op. 79, No. 2, *"Die Allmacht"*
92	Johannes Brahms, *Variations on a Theme by Handel*
94	J. S. Bach, *Well Tempered Clavier*, Book I, Prelude II
95–97	Friedrich Chopin, *Prelude No. 20* (C minor)
98	Robert Schumann, *Piano Concerto*, Op. 54
99	Anton Bruckner, *Symphony No. 7*, I
101–104	Friedrich Chopin, *Prelude No. 10* (C-sharp minor)
106	Friedrich Chopin, *Prelude No. 20* (C minor)
110	Friedrich Chopin, *Prelude No. 20* (C minor)
111–112	Johannes Brahms, *Variations on a Theme by Handel*
113–115	(tonal operations)
116	(array material)

S23

2	Arnold Schoenberg, *Quartet No. 4*
3–4	J. S. Bach, *Well Tempered Clavier*, Book I, Prelude I
8–9	W. A. Mozart, *Symphony No. 40*, II
10–16	J. S. Bach, *Well Tempered Clavier*, Book I, Fugue II
17–20	Richard Wagner, *Tristan und Isolde*, Vorspiel
22–23	Richard Wagner, *Tristan und Isolde*, Vorspiel
24–26	Robert Schumann, *Dichterliebe*, Op. 48, No. 1
27–33	Robert Schumann, *Dichterliebe*, Op. 48, No. 2
35	Ludwig van Beethoven, *Sonata*, Op. 27, No. 2

S24

1–3	W. A. Mozart, *Sonata in A major*, K. 331
4	Ludwig van Beethoven, *Sonata*, Op. 2, No. 1, Menuetto
6	W. A. Mozart, *Quartet in D minor*, K. 421
7–14	Ludwig van Beethoven, *Sonata*, Op. 109, II

15	W. A. Mozart, *Quartet in D minor*, K. 421
16–21	Ludwig van Beethoven, Sonata, Op. 109, II
22	Arnold Schoenberg, Op. 14, No. 2, *"In diesen Wintertagen"*
25	Friedrich Chopin, *Nocturne in G minor*, Op. 39, No. 1
26	W. A. Mozart, *Sonata in A major*, K. 331
28	J. S. Bach, *Well Tempered Clavier*, Book I, Prelude I
29–35	Friedrich Chopin, *Nocturne in G minor*, Op. 39, No. 1
36	Friedrich Chopin, *Nocturne in F-sharp minor*, p. 48, No. 2
38–46	Richard Wagner, *Tristan und Isolde*, Vorspiel
47	John Eaton, *Holy Sonnets of John Donne*, IV

S25
1	Ludwig van Beethoven, *Sonata*, Op. 109, II

S26   *Pierpont Variations*

S27
2–5	Anton Bruckner, *Symphony No. 7*, I
6	Robert Schumann, *Dichterliebe*, Op. 48, No. 2
8–10	Friedrich Chopin, *Ballade in G-minor*
15	Ludwig van Beethoven, *Sonata*, Op. 23 ("Waldstein"), I
16	J. S. Bach, *Mass in B minor*, "Christe Eleison"
17–19	J. S. Bach, *Mass in B minor*, "Domine Deus"
22	Johannes Brahms, *Variations on a Theme by Haydn*
24–25	Friedrich Chopin, *Ballade in G-minor*
27	Anton Bruckner, *Symphony No. 7*, I
32	J. S. Bach, *Well Tempered Clavier*, Book I, Prelude II
33–35	Anton Bruckner, *Symphony No. 7*, I
43	Arnold Schoenberg, *Quartet No. 4*

S28   (unknown work)

S29   *Orchestra Piece*

S30
1–6	*Pierpont Variations*
7	Ludwig van Beethoven, *Sonata*, Op. 27, No. 2
9	*Pierpont Variations*

S31
1	Ludwig van Beethoven, *Concerto for Piano No. 4*, Op. 58
3	Franz Schubert, Op. 79, No. 2, *"Die Allmacht"*
6	Ludwig van Beethoven, *Bagatelle*, Op. 126, No. 1
7	Richard Wagner, *Tristan und Isolde*, Vorspiel

Library of Congress Cataloging in Publication Data

Kuhn, Reinhard Clifford.
   The demon of noontide.

   Bibliography: p.
   Includes index.
   1.   Boredom in literature.   I.   Title.
PN56.B7K8   809'.933'53   76-3269
ISBN 0-691-06311-7